Allan Ramsay

Twayne's English Authors Series

Bertram H. Davis, Editor
Florida State University

TEAS 400

ALLAN RAMSAY (1684–1758)
Portrait by William Aikman
Reproduced by kind permission of the
Scottish National Portrait Gallery,
Edinburgh, Scotland

Allan Ramsay

By Allan H. MacLaine

University of Rhode Island

Twayne Publishers • *Boston*

Allan Ramsay

Allan H. MacLaine

Copyright © 1985 by G. K. Hall & Company
All Rights Reserved
Published by Twayne Publishers
A Division of G. K. Hall & Company
70 Lincoln Street
Boston, Massachusetts 02111

Book Production by Elizabeth Todesco

Book Design by Barbara Anderson

Printed on permanent/durable acid-free
paper and bound in the United States of
America.

**Library of Congress Cataloging in
Publication Data**

MacLaine, Allan H.
  Allan Ramsay.

  (Twayne's English authors series; TEAS 400)
  Bibliography: p. 152
  Includes index.
  1. Ramsay, Allan, 1685–1758—
Criticism and interpretation.
  I. Title. II. Series.
  PR3657.M25 1985   821'.5   84–15763
  ISBN 0–8057–6886–6

For Stacy, with love

Contents

About the Author

Allan H. MacLaine, professor of English at the University of Rhode Island, is a leading authority on the Scots poetic tradition. Born in Montreal and educated at McGill and Brown universities, he taught in both of these institutions, at the University of Massachusetts, and at Texas Christian University. From 1966 to 1967 he served as chairman of the English Department, and from 1967 to 1971 as dean of the Division of University Extension at the University of Rhode Island.

His books, besides *Allan Ramsay,* are *The Student's Comprehensive Guide to the Canterbury Tales* (1964), *The Christis Kirk Tradition: Its Evolution in Scots Poetry to Burns* (in four installments in *Studies in Scottish Literature,* 1964–65), and *Robert Fergusson* (1965). He is also the author of a long introductory essay for *The Beginnings to 1558,* the first volume of *Great Writers Student Library* (1980). Of Dr. MacLaine's twenty-six other essays and articles published in various scholarly journals in Britain and the United States, twenty deal with the history and criticism of Scottish poetry.

Currently, Dr. MacLaine is completing a major critical study of the work of Robert Burns.

Preface

Allan Ramsay is an eighteenth-century poet of extraordinary interest who has been generally undervalued in recent times, both in criticism and in literary histories. One obvious reason for this is the fact that Ramsay wrote all of his significant poetry in Scots, a language that presents some difficulties (not severe ones) for modern readers. Secondly, he has been overshadowed by the towering figure of his successor Burns, so that for most people today Scots poetry *is* Burns, and Ramsay, if he is known at all, is remembered only as a shadowy "forerunner," seldom as a poet in his own right. Apart from Burns, indeed, the entire, fascinating poetic tradition of Scotland is largely unknown territory; and it has only been within the last couple of decades that Scottish poetry has begun to be recognized as an important, partially independent branch of British literature. As a consequence of all these factors, even a quite remarkable poet like Ramsay has suffered from undeserved neglect. This is the first full-length critical study of his work.

During the two and one half centuries that have passed since Ramsay's busily productive years his literary reputation has fluctuated wildly. In his own lifetime (1684–1758), through the eighteenth century, and well into the nineteenth, Ramsay enjoyed a broad-based popularity in his native country, and even in England and Ireland, chiefly by virtue of the fame of his pastoral comedy, *The Gentle Shepherd.* With the learned and snobbish critics of the later eighteenth century, however, he did not fare so well, and was often charged with "vulgarity." After the spectacular success of Burns, which made Scots poetry respectable even in the most rarified literary circles, Ramsay was suddenly boosted to critical acclaim. The biographical account of George Chalmers and the glowing critical essay of Lord Woodhouselee, published in 1800 in a new handsome edition of Ramsay's poems, mark the beginning of serious, scholarly study of his work. Through most of the nineteenth century that followed his work was generally overpraised by sentimental, nationalistic critics. But in 1898 the critical tide turned against him once more, with the old charge of "vulgarity" brought up again by Thomas F. Henderson. Consequently, in the twentieth century Ramsay's status has tended to be downgraded in literary history and criticism, though recently there have been clear signs that the pendulum is beginning to swing the other way, and that a new and fairer view of Ramsay is starting to emerge.

The most convincing evidence of a new, serious view of Ramsay was the publication in six volumes of the splendid Scottish Text Society edition of Ramsay's *Works* (1945–74), with the first two volumes edited by Burns Martin and John W. Oliver, the last four by Alexander M. Kinghorn and Alexander Law. This is by far the most ambitious piece of Ramsay scholarship ever to appear, and it augurs a brighter future for Ramsay's literary reputation. Particularly significant is Dr. Kinghorn's biographical and critical study in volume 4. In terms of critical analysis, however, Kinghorn's treatment is very incomplete: he concentrates on three or four aspects of Ramsay's work, but largely ignores his satires, epistles, and other genres central to his life's work. The present study is, among other things, an effort to fill that gap, and to make available the first truly comprehensive, thorough, book-length treatment of Allan Ramsay's poetry.

My large debt to previous commentators on Ramsay is, I hope, adequately acknowledged in the notes. In particular, I feel grateful (as must all students of Ramsay) for the pioneer studies of Burns Martin, David Daiches, Thomas Crawford, and, above all, Alexander Kinghorn. I owe something, also, to my own institution, the University of Rhode Island, for a sabbatical leave that enabled me to complete the research for this book. Thanks are due, further, to Mrs. Ethel Thompson, for expert work in typing a difficult manuscript. Finally, I wish to express my deepest gratitude to my wife, Stacy Lagerquist MacLaine, who has been supportive in many ways, and has patiently read with keen critical intelligence every word of the manuscript as it progressed. To her this book is lovingly inscribed.

Allan H. MacLaine

University of Rhode Island

Chronology

1684   Allan Ramsay born in Leadhills, Lanarkshire, Scotland, son of John Ramsay, supervisor of lead mines. Probably attended nearby parish school at Crawfordmoor.

1700   Moves to Edinburgh in that year or shortly thereafter.

1704   Apprenticed to an Edinburgh wigmaker.

1710   Completes apprenticeship and is enrolled as a "burgess" of Edinburgh.

1712   Establishes his own wigmaker's shop, probably in the Grassmarket of Edinburgh. Joins the Easy Club of young nationalists, founded in May. Begins writing poems in Scots and English, including, "Elegy on Maggy Johnston." Marries Christian Ross on 14 December.

1713   Birth of the poet's eldest son, Allan, the first of five or six children.

1715   Writes "Christis Kirk on the Green," canto 2, a sequel to the original medieval poem. Probably also composes "A Tale of Three Bonnets," a political satire, and other pieces. Easy Club disbanded.

1718   Moves his shop to High Street of Edinburgh, opposite Niddry's Wynd, and begins to shift from wigmaking to bookselling and publishing as his major business. Begins publishing his own poems and songs in pamphlet or broadside form. Borrows the Bannatyne Manuscript of Middle Scots poetry, which later becomes the basis of his anthology, *The Ever Green.*

1721   Publishes by subscription a handsome collected volume of *Poems by Allan Ramsay.*

1722   Moves his shop to High Street opposite the Cross-Well. Publishes first set of *Fables and Tales.*

1723   *Tea-Table Miscellany,* volume 1, an anthology of Scots songs.

1724   Admitted (as honorary member) to Royal Company

of Archers, an exclusive Edinburgh association, as "Bard." *The Ever Green,* 2 volumes, an anthology of Middle Scots Poetry.

1725 Final move of bookshop to the High Street at the east end of the Luckenbooths, where he also establishes the first "circulating library" in Great Britain. *The Gentle Shepherd,* a pastoral comedy.

1726 *Tea-Table Miscellany,* volume 2.

1727 *Tea-Table Miscellany,* volume 3.

1728 Publishes by subscription second collected volume of *Poems by Allan Ramsay.*

1729 Helps to establish "Academy of St. Luke," a school for painting and drawing in Edinburgh.

1730 *Collection of Thirty Fables.*

1734 *The Gentle Shepherd,* sixth edition, with songs added.

1736 Opens theater in Carrubber's Close, Edinburgh.

1737 *Tea-Table Miscellany,* volume 4.

1739 Forced to close theater.

1740 Retires from active business to live in his fine new house, the "Goose-Pie," on Castlehill, Edinburgh.

1743 Wife dies.

1758 Ramsay dies at Edinburgh in January, at age seventy-four.

Chapter One

"Honest Allan" Ramsay and the Scots Poetic Tradition

When Allan Ramsay first emerged from obscurity about 1715, the vernacular literature of Scotland was at a low ebb indeed; yet within a couple of decades Ramsay succeeded, almost single-handedly, in reinvigorating the Scots poetic tradition and in laying the essential foundations for modern Scottish poetry. Specifically, he gave to the eighteenth-century Scots revival both its original impetus and its final direction. In the process of this remarkable achievement Ramsay rose to national fame, and acquired the affectionate nickname of "honest Allan."[1]

Why "honest" Allan? The phrase certainly did not signify that Ramsay was exceptionally scrupulous in his business dealings nor that he was invariably sincere in what he said or wrote. To understand the rather special meaning of this soubriquet we need to know something of the cultural situation in Scotland when Ramsay arrived on the scene—and to do that we must go back several centuries to review the evolution of Scots poetry up to his time.

Scottish Poetry Before Ramsay

The poetry of Scotland developed relatively late in the European perspective, the earliest masterpiece in the Middle Scots language dating about 1375.[2] This is the fine patriotic romance of *The Bruce* by John Barbour, celebrating the exploits of King Robert Bruce in the War of Independence against English domination. In the fifteenth and early sixteenth centuries, however, the Scottish court became the center of a brilliant national poetry, a poetry far superior in quality and sophistication to that produced in England during the same era. The forerunner of this Middle Scots "golden age" was a king himself, James I

(1394–1437), author of an accomplished love allegory called *The Kingis Quair* (The king's book) and perhaps also of two hilarious burlesque poems on peasant celebrations, "Peblis to the Play" and "Christis Kirk on the Green." The latter two became the prototypes of a highly distinctive Scottish genre that may be called the "Christis Kirk" tradition and that persisted for many centuries—until the present time, in fact.[3] The work of James I was followed by that of the truly great Middle Scots poets, or "makars" of the half century from about 1470 to 1520—namely, Robert Henryson (ca. 1425–ca. 1506), William Dunbar (ca. 1460–ca. 1522), and Gavin Douglas (1475–1522). In the writings of these men, Blind Harry (ca. 1450–92), and other lesser lights, Scots poetry attained a peak of power and brilliance that was not to be reached again until the work of Robert Burns three hundred years later. After Douglas, the Middle Scots poetic tradition gradually declined in the course of the sixteenth century, though impressive and distinguished work continued to be produced for two more generations, especially by Sir David Lindsay (ca. 1490–1555), Alexander Scott (ca. 1515–83), and Alexander Montgomerie (ca. 1540–ca. 1610).

The significant history of Middle Scots poetry, then, extends over a period of roughly two centuries—from the work of Barbour (ca. 1375) to that of Montgomerie (ca. 1585). Generally speaking, the poetry produced in Scotland during these centuries falls into three broad categories. First of all, there was courtly poetry, ornate and sophisticated in style, with its "termes aureate," consisting of romances, love allegories, dream-visions, love lyrics, moral allegories, and elaborate instructional works on political and religious subjects. This poetry was late medieval and international in character, though expressed in a distinctive Scots literary language. Representative of this very extensive group are Barbour's *Bruce, The Kingis Quair* of James I, Henryson's *Testament of Cresseid,* Dunbar's "The Golden Targe," Douglas's superb translation of Virgil's *Aeneid,* the love lyrics of Alexander Scott, Montgomerie's *The Cherrie and the Slae,* as well as many of the poems of Lindsay and of numerous anonymous writers. Secondly, at the other end of the social scale, there was oral folk poetry consisting of popular ballads and songs—a vibrant tradition that flourished mightily during these centuries. Finally, there was a third and very important classification which might be called art poetry on folk themes. Into this large category fall such pieces as "Christis Kirk" and "Peblis," Henryson's *Fables,* much of the best work of Dunbar, Lindsay, and others, Scott's "Justing and Debait," and a great bulk of poems by unknown authors. Of these three broad types of poetry the first, the courtly, simply died with the Middle Ages, but the other two persisted into modern times.

Thus, for over two hundred years Scotland had a vigorous and versatile poetry in the native Middle Scots tongue. Much of it was centered in the court at Edinburgh, but many facets of the tradition had deep roots in the common people and in the middle class. It was a genuine national literature, often brilliant, and occasionally rising to artistic greatness. In the course of the seventeenth century, however, Scots poetry went into a steep, almost fatal, decline.

Why did this drastic fading of the old tradition occur? Among many possible causes, three or four may be adduced as certain. One was the triumph of Knoxian Calvinism, which proscribed poetry along with other "lewd" entertainments, bringing such powerful pressure to bear as to virtually stifle the creation of new art poetry in Scotland (except among a handful of the aristocracy). A second severe blow was the removal in 1603 of the court, which had always been the center of poetic patronage, from Edinburgh to London. Furthermore, the overwhelming influence of the great English poetry of the late sixteenth and seventeenth centuries persuaded the few Scottish gentlemen who continued to practice the art to turn their backs upon the native tradition and to follow the Elizabethan English style. The result was an almost complete break in the development of sophisticated poetry in the Scots tongue, though the folk poetry continued to thrive in oral transmission despite the Kirk's disapproval. From the whole seventeenth century only a handful of new art poems in Scots have come down to us, written by country gentlemen of the type of the Sempills of Beltrees. Among these sporadic efforts "The Life and Death of Habbie Simson" (ca. 1640) by Robert Sempill of Beltrees was the prototype of the comic-elegy genre, which became immensely popular in the next century. But, on the whole, the seventeenth century is a dismal hiatus in the history of Scots poetry. By the year 1700

the Scots tongue had fallen out of use as a versatile literary
language and had come to be employed for comic purposes
only. It was as though the nation had forgotten that it had once
had a great literature. Scots poetry had become little more than
a "literary joke."[4]

In the opening decade of the eighteenth century, however,
a dramatic reversal of this situation began to gather strength.
The primary stimulus of this Scots revival was a political event,
the parliamentary Union of 1707 with England. By this single
act the Scottish parliament voted itself out of existence, the
thousand-year history of Scotland as a sovereign state came to
an end, and, politically, Scotland was reduced to the status of
an English province. Naturally, the nation was deeply divided
over this issue. Almost certainly a majority of the people was
opposed to the Union, but the politicians passed it by a vote
of about two to one, some of them seduced by "English gold,"
others by the promise of economic advantages to come from
an expanded market for Scottish goods. At any rate, the Union
provoked a profound cultural reaction. Many Scots, suffering
from a feeling of injured dignity and political betrayal, were
stirred to reassert their country's ancient cultural identity and
to resist assimilation by England. One form that this resurgence
of Scottish nationalism took was a renewed interest in Scots
poetry.

The first sign of the new movement was the publication by
James Watson, an Edinburgh printer, of an epoch-making anthology, *A Choice Collection of Comic and Serious Scots Poems, both Antient
and Modern,* in three volumes dated 1706, 1709, and 1711.
This remarkable work, the very publication of which is evidence
that a reading public for Scots verse did in fact exist, is strangely
mixed in content. Watson included a few specimens of Middle
Scots, transcribed from inaccurate seventeenth-century printings
("Christis Kirk" has the place of honor as the first poem in
the first volume), a number of poems in English by Scotsmen,
several seventeenth-century popular pieces ("Habbie Simson"
among them), and, most significantly, various new productions
in Scots. Among the last group the most notable item is by
William Hamilton of Gilbertfield (near Glasgow), a retired army
officer, whose contribution in the six-line "Habbie" stanza—
"The Last Dying Words of Bonny Heck, a Famous Greyhound

in the Shire of Fife"—marks the beginning of a new comic poetry in Scots. Hamilton also published elsewhere a handful of fairly lively songs in Scots, inaugurated a famous exchange of verse letters with Allan Ramsay in 1719, and in 1722 produced a "translation" of Blind Harry's long Middle Scots poem, *Wallace,* into crabbed English couplets which, despite their pedestrian quality, were destined to inspire the youthful Burns half a century later.[5] By virtue of "Bonny Heck," Hamilton of Gilbertfield is the first significant poet in the field of the eighteenth-century Scots revival.

The movement inaugurated by Watson and Hamilton was immediately taken over by the versatile Allan Ramsay. Beginning about 1712, Ramsay produced a steady stream of poems in Scots (as well as many in English); at the same time he labored indefatigably as publisher, anthologist, and propagandist for the native poetic tradition. In *The Ever Green* (1724) he produced an invaluable and ambitious collection of Middle Scots poetry that far surpassed that of Watson, and in the hugely popular *Tea-Table Miscellany* (begun in 1723) he made available hundreds of traditional Scots songs while also providing a medium for publication of new work in the same genre. Important as these latter activities were, by and large Ramsay's own original poetry in Scots was even more influential in launching the Scots vernacular revival of the eighteenth century.

The tradition that Ramsay inherited was clearly an impoverished one. The very names of the great makars of the past were half forgotten; their works (except for a modest sampling in Watson's *Choice Collection*) survived mainly in obscure and scattered manuscripts. Though Scots continued to be spoken in everyday use among all social classes in Ramsay's time, most of the aristocracy and literati of Edinburgh had shifted to standard English for writing purposes. For serious literary work the native tongue had been abandoned for over a century and had come to be used for comic poems only, specifically for jocular pieces depicting low life. Ramsay set out to change all this. He aimed at reviving many of the older genres and demonstrating their continued vitality and adaptability for modern uses. In choosing to write in Scots himself Ramsay was taking something of a risk, swimming (to a degree at least) against prevailing cultural currents. The literary and linguistic pressures of English influence, especially among the upper classes in Scotland, were powerful indeed. Yet Ramsay saw an opportunity in the new surge of Scottish nationalism that resulted from the Union, and, motivated by a genuine patriotism, he exploited this tendency with great skill. He came to be called "honest Allan" because he stood for the old-fashioned, sturdy Scottish values in opposition to foreign affectations—above all, because he wrote in "plain braid Scots," the familiar and beloved tongue of the people. And in his campaign to reestablish a Scots national poetry, Ramsay, shrewd and talented as he was, achieved a remarkable historic success. Let us turn now to a more detailed consideration of this extraordinary career.[6]

The Life of Allan Ramsay

Allan Ramsay was born in the desolate village of Leadhills in the hill country of southwestern Lanarkshire in 1684 (or possibly 1685), only about twenty-five miles to the east of Mauchline in Ayrshire where Burns was to produce his first great volume of poems almost exactly a century later. His father, John Ramsay, was an obscure middle-class superintendent of the lead mines there for the Earl of Hopeton; his mother was an Englishwoman from Derbyshire. When Ramsay was in his infancy his father died, his mother remarried, and Allan was brought up as a rural boy herding sheep in a wild countryside. What formal schooling he received must have taken place in the parish school of the neighboring village of Crawfordmoor, six miles away.

About 1700 or shortly thereafter Ramsay left his home village and moved to Edinburgh where he was apprenticed to a wigmaker in 1704; on 19 July 1710, having completed the six-year apprenticeship, he was enrolled as a "burgess" of Edinburgh, and apparently set up in business for himself. Except for the bare fact that he was involved in the trade of wigmaking, Ramsay's first ten years in Edinburgh (1700–1710) are totally obscure. Beginning with 1710, however, the records of his life story become fairly copious. On 14 December 1712, by then established in business, Ramsay married a local woman, Christian Ross, with whom he enjoyed a long and happy union and by whom he had at least five children (including his eldest son,

Allan Ramsay, Jr., who became a celebrated portrait painter). Ramsay's business career is generally well documented. Traditionally, his first wigmaking shop, probably set up in 1712, was in the Grassmarket in the west end of the city. By 1718, however, he had moved to the eastern part of the High Street, "at the sign of the Mercury, opposite Niddry's Wynd," and had shifted his main occupation (no doubt by degrees) from that of a wigmaker to that of a bookseller and publisher. Thereafter, as his prosperity increased, Ramsay relocated his establishment twice more, gradually moving up the slope of the High Street (both physically and socially) into the very heart of the city. In 1722 he moved from Niddry's Wynd to a shop in the High Street "at the sign of the Mercury opposite the Cross-Well," and, finally, from there in 1725 to his final location in "the East-end of the Luckenbooths" adjacent to the High Kirk of St. Giles.[7] By then Ramsay's bookshop had become a thriving business, the chief focal point of the literary life of the old town of Edinburgh, and Ramsay himself had achieved national celebrity as a poet and a resounding commercial success as bookseller and publisher.

The "rags to riches" pattern of Ramsay's business career suggests qualities of shrewdness, energy, and versatile talent that are paralleled in his development as a creative artist. His poetic work falls into three periods: from about 1712 to 1721 (when the first major edition of his *Poems* appeared); from 1721 to 1728 (a second volume of *Poems*); and from 1728 until his death in 1758.

The considerable range of Ramsay's original work as a poet is clearly apparent in the earliest phase of his career. Seemingly, he got his start as a poet through his membership in the Easy Club, a clique of young Scots nationalists founded in May 1712. These young men shared literary interests, and, until they disbanded in 1715, provided for Ramsay a sympathetic audience for his early poems. At the very beginning of his creative work (as throughout his life) Ramsay attempted to write both in fashionable neoclassical English and in vernacular Scots. One of his earliest major pieces is in genteel English, "The Morning Interview" (1716), a competent but pallid imitation of Pope's *Rape of the Lock*. This was followed by two other extensive poems in English heroic couplets, "Tartana" (1718) and "Content"

(1719), both of which suffer from a labored pretentiousness. Far more successful are his Scots poems, beginning with his ambitious sequels to the fifteenth-century "Christis Kirk on the Green"—cantos 2 and 3, published in 1718—which are quite brilliant and lively evocations of Scottish country life and customs. Since the Scots tongue had come to be used, as we have seen, only for comic treatment of low life, Ramsay naturally began as a Scots poet in this vein. In his continuations of "Christis Kirk" he not only gave new publicity to the Middle Scots poem, but he also showed the adaptability of the "Christis Kirk" tradition for modern purposes. At about the same time he composed "A Tale of Three Bonnets," a vigorous satire in braid Scots on the parliamentary Union of Scotland and England. This, Ramsay's most politically radical poem, was not published until 1722 and then anonymously. He then moved on to other Scots comic genres, producing in 1718 a series of comic elegies—"Maggie Johnston," "John Cowper," and "Lucky Wood"—all modeled on Sempill's "The Life and Death of Habbie Simson"; followed by "Lucky Spence's Last Advice" in the genre of Hamilton's "Bonny Heck." In 1719, initiated by Hamilton of Gilbertfield, came the series of Horatian verse epistles in the "Habbie" stanza which inaugurated a new Scottish genre that was to become very important in the Scots poetic revival, culminating in the great epistles of Burns.

In all of these early Scots efforts until 1719, Ramsay, with characteristic conservatism, stuck pretty much to various forms of comic verse. But in that year he began to move into more revolutionary experiments, using Scots for the first time since the sixteenth century for serious poetry in "Richy and Sandy," a pastoral on the death of Joseph Addison. This was followed up in the next year by a love pastoral in Scots called "Patie and Roger" which was destined to become the germ of Ramsay's later masterpiece, the pastoral play of *The Gentle Shepherd* (1725). A little earlier (1718) Ramsay had begun to experiment in yet another genre, Scots songs, providing new or refurbished words for traditional tunes—an effort that was to lead to incalculable results, including the supreme achievements of Burns at the end of the century.

By 1720 Ramsay had acquired a reputation in Edinburgh and beyond as a new native poet of substantial talent. Because

he was himself a bookseller and publisher he was able to publish
and distribute his own poems in pamphlet or broadside form
as he composed them. Ramsay's two professions, in fact, rein-
forced one another: for his poetry he had ready access to publication and publicity, and at the same time his growing fame as
a poet brought increased trade to his bookstore. Most of his
early poems were issued separately as pamphlets, so that by
1720 he had enough material to put out a preliminary volume
of his *Poems,* a volume which consisted simply of a gathering
together of unsold copies of individual pamphlets. But in the
next year, 1721, Ramsay was able to publish by subscription
a full-blown, handsome collected edition of his work as *Poems
by Allan Ramsay,* including all of his significant work to date
(except for the daring "Tale of Three Bonnets"). The list of
subscribers included a majority of the enlightened gentry and
professional class of Edinburgh (whom Ramsay had assiduously
cultivated over the years), as well as scattered notables from
elsewhere in Scotland and even in England. Among those listed,
surprisingly enough, was a *"Mr.* Alexander Pope." In any event,
the volume, expensively produced and priced at a guinea a
copy, was a resounding success. In ten short but strenuous years
Allan Ramsay had risen from struggling wigmaker to national
poet.

In the second phase of his career, from 1721 to 1728, Ramsay
prospered in business and continued to expand his range as a
creative artist. In 1722 he published the first edition of his *Fables
and Tales,* consisting mainly of lively Scots adaptations of French
fables by La Motte and La Fontaine, but including a few of
his own invention. In the realm of pastoral poetry Ramsay labored fruitfully in these years. In 1721 appeared his second
pastoral elegy, "Robert, Richy, and Sandy," lamenting the death
of Matthew Prior; and in 1723 came "Jenny and Meggy," a
sequel to "Patie and Roger." These latter two pieces formed
the nucleus of *The Gentle Shepherd,* a full-length pastoral drama
published in 1725, which is Ramsay's largest and most important
work as an original poet. In 1728, after the phenomenal success
of John Gay's *The Beggar's Opera,* Ramsay was encouraged to
transform *The Gentle Shepherd* into a ballad opera by the addition
of some twenty songs scattered through the text; and in this
form his play enjoyed a huge popularity which lasted well into

the nineteenth century and assured Ramsay's permanent place in Scottish and British literary history.

During these same years Ramsay produced miscellaneous poetry in various genres, in both Scots and English, at a fairly steady pace. Like Burns after his first fame, Ramsay was often seduced from his natural creative bent and into the writing of occasional pieces to please various individuals or groups. His several poems extolling the Royal Company of Archers fall into this category, along with many pieces lamenting deaths or celebrating weddings and births among his aristocratic patrons and friends. Very much better are such poems as "The Last Speech of a Wretched Miser" or "The Monk and the Miller's Wife," the latter being a rich adaptation of the Middle Scots "The Freiris of Berwick."

Much of Ramsay's energy during the 1720s was diverted into his crucial work as an editor of Scots poetry. In 1723 he launched *The Tea-Table Miscellany* which was to grow over the years from one to four volumes and become the first important anthology of Scots songs. Ramsay included in this collection some genuine old folk songs and ballads, a much larger number of "modernized" lyrics (in English as well as Scots) for traditional tunes, and a fair number of wholly new songs (also to traditional tunes) by himself and by younger poets like Robert Crawford and William Hamilton of Bangour. The *Miscellany,* therefore, functioned to preserve the riches of the past and also to provide an outlet for new creative song writing. It turned out to be the most successful and lucrative of all Ramsay's publishing enterprises.

The Tea-Table Miscellany was immediately followed in 1724 by *The Ever Green,* a two-volume anthology of Middle Scots poetry largely transcribed from the Bannatyne Manuscript of 1568, which Ramsay was able to borrow from a wealthy friend. Though not nearly so popular as his song collection, *The Ever Green* has very great historical importance as the first large modern printing of the work of the medieval makars (immediately superseding Watson's fragmentary *Choice Collection*). In it Ramsay made easily available for the first time the great Scots poetry of the past. Though very imperfect from a scholarly point of view, *The Ever Green* was the pioneer anthology of Middle Scots, the first of a long series, and an admirable patriotic achievement.

Two further events in Ramsay's life during this period deserve mention. Probably about the time when Ramsay moved to his final bookshop in the Luckenbooths in 1725 he established as a sideline a "circulating library"—that is, a library where people could borrow books at a modest fee per day or week—which seems to have been the first of its kind in Great Britain. Ramsay's library soon came under criticism by rigid moralists in Edinburgh, but he weathered the storm, and the library continued to flourish under him and his successors for generations. Then, in 1728, Ramsay was able to publish, again by subscription, a second collected volume of *Poems by Allan Ramsay,* volume 2, which included *The Gentle Shepherd* (without the songs) and most of the new poetry Ramsay had written since the 1721 edition. This second volume was larger and, to judge by the list of subscribers, even more successful than the first; and it clearly established "honest Allan" as the respected and popular national poet of Scotland.

The third phase of Ramsay's creative career extends from 1728 until his death in 1758 at the ripe age of seventy-four. During the first dozen years of this period Ramsay continued in business in his bustling shop in the Luckenbooths until 1740 when he was rich enough to retire from active commercial life. During his last decade of business pursuits Ramsay became involved in a courageous attempt to establish a theater in Edinburgh to enhance the city's culture. In fact, he opened a theater in Carrubber's Close in 1736 with some initial success. In the next year, however, the unpopular Licensing Act forbidding commercial theaters outside of London was passed, creating immediate legal difficulties for Ramsay's venture. Moreover, Edinburgh's puritanical majority, opposed on moral grounds to any theaters, used the legal situation as a weapon to close down the house in Carrubber's Close. After three years of bitter struggle the bigots finally prevailed and Ramsay was forced to disband his company of actors in the spring of 1739. For the poet this was a frustrating but far from catastrophic defeat.

In 1740 Ramsay had built for himself the famous "Goose-Pie" house (so called from its octagonal shape) on the Castlehill, overlooking the North Loch with a fine view of the Firth of Forth and of Fife beyond. This house, which still exists on the little street now called Ramsay Gardens, was then in a semirural

location, though very close to the busy High Street. Here the
poet settled into a pleasant and comfortable life of literary leisure. A severe blow came in 1743 with the death of his wife;
but Ramsay himself lived on for another fifteen years, enjoying
his status as a celebrity, occasionally visiting the fine country
houses of his aristocratic friends, cheerfully entertaining in his
cozy "bower" on Castlehill, remaining to the end an active,
distinguished citizen of Auld Reekie—the crowded, battered
town that he loved.

It is a curious fact that during this long stretch of three decades
after 1728 Ramsay published almost no new poetry of his own,
though he continued to issue further editions of his earlier writings with undiminished energy until his retirement in 1740.
Writing to the painter John Smibert in May of 1736, he asserted
that "these six or seven years past I have not wrote a line of
poetry" (STS, 4:206). We know, however, that this statement
was misleading, since a very substantial quantity of *unpublished*
poems written after 1728 has survived.[8] Indeed, Ramsay continued to write quite prolifically through the last thirty years of
his life—but only for private circulation among his friends and
patrons, and for his own amusement. A few of these unpublished
poems of Ramsay's mature years are among his best, including
the charming "Epistle to John Wardlaw" (1736) and the moving
"Elegy in Memory of William Aikman" (1731).

Why this surprising reluctance to publish? Perhaps Ramsay
felt that he had made his name and fortune and now saw no
further economic need to publish more original poetry, or, as
he put it to Smibert, to "risk the reputation I had acquired."
A statement in the "Life of Allan Ramsay" attributed to his
son (Allan Ramsay the Younger), however, throws a somewhat
different light on the matter. According to this account Ramsay,
when urged by one of his friends to give more of his work to
the public, replied that *"he was more inclined . . . to recall much
of what he had already given; and that if half his printed works
were burnt, the other half, like the Sybill's books, would become more
valuable by it"* (STS, 4:74). This comment suggests that Ramsay's
earlier and (to modern readers) irritating habit of self-praise
was simply part of his long public relations effort to achieve
fame, a mere facade that the poet himself did not really believe
in, and that, at least in his middle age, Ramsay had acquired

a healthy critical judgment as to the permanent value of his own work. Nevertheless, in this later unpublished work, among large amounts of trivia and slapdash experiments, there are several fine poems that are actually superior artistically to many of Ramsay's earlier pieces that he printed and apparently set considerable store by. Like most writers Ramsay obviously had difficulty in seeing his own work in a clear or objective light.

Altogether, Allan Ramsay's life was a large success. Lacking genius, he made the most of his considerable talents. By shrewd management, discreet living, and persistent effort, Ramsay gradually built a solid prosperity that made possible his realization of the Horatian dream of literary leisure in a long, cheerful old age—a dream that was to elude his successors, Fergusson and Burns. More importantly, in his many-faceted literary work both as author and editor Ramsay laid the indispensable foundation for the Scots poetic revival of the eighteenth century. To that cause he was wholly and selflessly dedicated. Motivated by a genuine patriotism, Ramsay built bridges to the future. As Professor Kinghorn says (*STS,* 14:169), no other in his generation was as deserving of the proud title of "Scots poet."

In the chapters that follow Ramsay's work as a man of letters will be considered in detail. Fortunately, his entire writings lend themselves to easy division into genres as follows: Scots satires, Scots epistles and odes (partially modeled on Horace), Scots pastorals, Scots songs, fables and tales, poems in English. In this study a chapter will be devoted to each of these topics, with the materials treated in chronological order within each genre, followed by a chapter on Ramsay's work as anthologist and propagandist and a final one summing up his total achievement in both a critical and historical perspective.

Chapter Two

Scots Satires

At the very beginning of his poetic career Allan Ramsay made the conscious but risky decision of writing in his native Scottish tongue and of attempting to breathe new life into the moribund Scots poetic tradition. That tradition, as we have noted in the previous chapter, had become so impoverished that by Ramsay's time the Scots language was used only for humorous treatments of low life. It was, therefore, wholly natural if not inevitable that Ramsay should launch his career as a Scots poet by turning to various types of comic verse at the outset. He began with two major efforts in satiric verse—social satire in his continuations of "Christis Kirk on the Green" and political satire in "A Tale of Three Bonnets." At about the same time he moved into another popular comic form, the Scots comic elegy, producing no fewer than six of these from 1712 onward. Another traditional Scots satiric form, the "mock testament," attracted him also, and he tried his hand at two or three other types of comic verse in the vernacular. Altogether, Ramsay produced over fifteen satiric poems in Scots, most of them early in his career, including several of his finest efforts.

"Christis Kirk on the Green," Cantos 2 and 3

Ramsay's two supplemental cantos of "Christis Kirk on the Green," nearly 400 lines in all, are his most sustained effort in Scots except for *The Gentle Shepherd* and "A Tale of Three Bonnets." Of his many poems in English, only "Content" and "Health" are longer. These cantos, therefore, must be regarded among his major works, and yet they have been strangely neglected by the critics. Lord Woodhouselee, it is true, devotes some four laudatory pages to them—"a composition of very high merit"—but his discussion is largely summary, with minimal critical analysis.[1] Among modern critics, Burns Martin praises Ramsay's handling of the stanza form, David Daiches and David Craig stress the self-conscious antiquarianism of the work, but none of them pays more than cursory attention to it.[2] Most unaccountably, Kinghorn in his otherwise admirable critical treatment of Ramsay's poetry (*STS,* 4:90–152) ignores "Christis Kirk" altogether. Yet the two cantos represent, as we shall see, an ambitious and solid achievement.

For his inspiration Ramsay looked backward some three centuries to the original "Christis Kirk on the Green." George Bannatyne, the Edinburgh lawyer who compiled in 1568 a massive and invaluable manuscript anthology of Middle Scots poetry, ascribed the poem to King James I of Scotland (died 1437) and it probably is by him. At any rate, the fifteenth-century "Christis Kirk" became the prototype of an extremely popular, distinctively Scottish genre. In this type of poem we have a genial, satiric depiction of a lower-class celebration, such as a wedding, a fair, or a country dance, as seen from the point of view of an amused, superior onlooker. The poem normally begins with a panorama of the whole uproarious scene of merrymaking, drunkenness, and horseplay, followed by a series of vignettes highlighting the antics of individual characters amid the general confusion. There is considerable use of dialogue in the separate scenes, scenes that have a cumulative effect in building a vivid impression of the affair as a whole. In "Christis Kirk" and its companion piece, "Peblis to the Play," this formula is embodied in a distinctive and rollicking verse form, the "Christis Kirk" stanza, consisting of eight lines of alternating iambic tetrameter and trimeter with a rhyme scheme of *a b a b a b a b,* followed by a "bobwheel" of a very short line (monometer) and a trimeter refrain at the end. In the fifteenth-century prototypes a fairly consistent pattern of alliteration is superimposed, adding to the intricacy of this very difficult verse form.

The original "Christis Kirk" became very popular during the Middle Scots period, influencing the work of William Dunbar, Sir David Lindsay, Alexander Scott, and others of the Scots makars. In his hilarious poem called "The Justing and Debait" (ca. 1575), Scott fused the "Christis Kirk" tradition with another medieval genre, the "mock tournament," and modified the basic

verse form slightly by using a refrain line ending always in
the words "that day" or "that night." During the long winter
of the seventeenth century "Christis Kirk," almost alone among
Middle Scots art poems, retained its popularity and was reprinted
several times.[3] It was only natural, then, that this famous poem
should be a favorite of the eighteenth-century revivalists. James
Watson gave "Christis Kirk" the place of honor in his *Choice
Collection* (1706), and Allan Ramsay took it under his wing a
few years later.

Ramsay's earliest known editions of "Christis Kirk" are both
dated 1718; the first of these reprints the old poem as canto
1 with a sequel by Ramsay as canto 2; the second repeats these
cantos and adds a further sequel, canto 3. In his prefatory note
to canto 2 in the three-canto edition, Ramsay states that he
composed canto 2 in 1715 and canto 3 in 1718, so that it seems
probable that there was an earlier publication (now lost) of
the two-canto version before 1718 (see *STS,* 6:32). Ramsay
further asserts in his introductory note to canto 1 that he took
the text of the fifteenth-century poem "from an old Manuscript
Collection of *Scots Poems* written 150 Years ago" (*STS,* 1:57)—
that is, from the Bannatyne Manuscript. This statement is clearly
inaccurate since the text Ramsay printed is not the Bannatyne
version but is basically the corrupt text published in Watson's
Choice Collection. What certainly happened is that Ramsay prepared his two-canto edition before he had access to Bannatyne,
and he simply copied the old poem straight from Watson, including Watson's erroneous attribution of the work to King James
V. Sometime between the publication of the two-canto and the
three-canto versions Ramsay was able to borrow the Bannatyne
Manuscript; from it he changed the authorship to King James
I and made some other (largely minor) revisions. But even in
his final three-canto version the text of canto 1 is still predomi-
nantly Watson's rather than Bannatyne's. One evidence of this
is the fact that Ramsay, both in his printing of the old poem
and in his own sequels, adopted the simplified stanza form that
he found in Watson—a shortening of the two-line "bobwheel"
into a single dimeter tag line ending in "that day." Watson
undoubtedly derived his text from one of the corrupt seventeenth-century printings of the poem, such as that of Bishop
Edmund Gibson (1691) where the shortened bobwheel also

appears.[4] Where and when this version of the stanza originated remains a mystery, though it surely was suggested by Alexander Scott's "that day" refrain in "The Justing and Debait." Kinghorn and Law are mistaken in asserting (*STS*, 6:32) that Ramsay himself "altered" the stanza;[5] he just took it as he found it in Watson.

The original "Christis Kirk" describes a gathering of rustics on some festive occasion. A fight breaks out between two of the young men over a girl, leading to a kind of burlesque archery contest to decide the issue, and finally to a barbarous and drunken free-for-all involving the entire male population of the village. The poem seems to be a fragment, though the final stanza (there are twenty-four in all) begins with the words "When a' was done." Ramsay assumes that the work is incomplete and that the occasion of the festivities described was a wedding, though there is no indication of this in the text. His attempt to "complete" a famous poem such as this, already three centuries old, was indeed a daring one, fraught with potential pitfalls. Fortunately, Ramsay did not try to imitate the language and to write in Middle Scots. (His knowledge of that tongue was certainly shaky, as nearly all critics have noted, though not nearly so bad as some have suggested.) Rather, Ramsay's sequels are in more or less contemporary Scots, but sprinkled with proverbial sayings or "quaint" phrases that detract from its naturalness. Beyond that, Ramsay drags into the poem descriptions of old-fashioned folk rituals, such as the "bedding of the bride" and the "riding of the stang," to such an extent that he felt it necessary to add a set of footnotes to his poem to explain these old customs and quaint sayings. Daiches, Craig, and others are right in deploring the studied antiquarianism of Ramsay's sequels; his cantos suffer artistically from this sort of forced folklore in precisely the same way that Burns's "Halloween" suffers. But that is not the whole story of Ramsay's "Christis Kirk"; his cantos have some fine redeeming qualities, as a close look at the text will show.

Ramsay opens canto 1 (*STS*, 1:66–73) with a really brilliant transitional stanza:

| But there had been mair Blood and Skaith, | *more; injury*[6] |
| Sair Harship and great Spulie, | *sore hardship; injury* |

And mony a ane had gotten his Death
  By this unsonsie Tooly: *unhappy fight*
But that the bauld Good-wife of *Braith*   *bold*
  Arm'd wi' a great Kail Gully,   *cabbage knife*
Cam bellyflaught, and loot an Aith,   *swooping down; oath*
  She'd gar them a' be hooly   *make; quiet*
      Fou fast that Day.   *full*

Here Ramsay takes skillful advantage of the rollicking rhythm of the "Christis Kirk" stanza to bring the general brawl to a swift and dramatic end. The light, tricksy effect of the feminine rhymes in the trimeter lines helps with this, as does the sudden slowing down of the tempo in the final tag-line. At the same time, the formidable figure of the "Good-wife of *Braith*," with amusing folklore associations, is an ideal means of bringing about the truce. In this stanza Ramsay succeeds in catching much of the rambunctious and witty spirit of the original. It would indeed be difficult to imagine a more effective way of bridging the gap between the old poem and the new.

Though the rest of canto 2 does not quite live up to the brilliance of the opening stanza, Ramsay does maintain a brisk and entertaining pace. In stanzas 3 and 4 he presents contrasting vignettes of two characters carried over from the old poem, *"Hutchon"* (brave) and *"Tam Taylor"* (cowardly), in their different reactions to the truce. As in the Middle Scots original, Ramsay makes effective satiric use of the themes of peasant cowardice and bungling. In the next stanza a minstrel is brought in to provide music for dancing, and then, in stanza 6, Ramsay gives us a scene of uproarious farce as one of the young men approaches a girl with strenuous directness:

Claud Peky was na very blate,   *shy*
  He stood nae lang a dreigh;   *at a distance*
For by the Wame he gripped *Kate,*   *belly*
  And gar'd her gi'e a Skreigh: *made; squeel*
Had aff, quoth she, ye filthy Slate,   *hold off; sloven*
  Ye stink o' Leeks, O figh!
Let gae my Hands, I say, be quait;   *go; quiet*
  And wow gin she was skeigh,   *if; skittish*
      And mim that Day.   *affectedly modest*

This stanza probably owes something to a passage in Chaucer's
Miller's Tale (lines 3271–87) where Nicholas's initial wooing
of Alisoun is described; but in any case Ramsay's handling of
the scene is very skillful. He strikes just the right note of hilarious
burlesque, with swift movement and funny dialogue.

In his next dozen stanzas or so Ramsay presents a series of
dancing scenes that are lively and convincing. The middle lines
of stanza 10, for example, are wonderfully vivid:

The Lasses bab'd about the Reel,	*danced* (*bobbed*)
Gar'd a' their Hurdies wallop,	*made; buttocks*
And swat like Pownies whan they speel	*sweat; ponies; climb*
Up Braes, or when they gallop. . . .	*hills*

What better way to suggest the sensual, sweaty bouncing of a
reel than in these brief lines? This is Ramsay at his earthy,
colloquial best. Many more such examples could easily be drawn
from canto 2, but the passages cited above are perhaps enough
to suggest the vigorous quality of the whole. In the latter part
of this canto Ramsay goes on to depict various excesses of eating
and drinking at the party, and finally the coming of evening
and the ceremonial "bedding" of the bride.

Canto 3 opens with a whimsical description of daybreak the
next morning when the sleepy villagers "Begoud to rax and
rift" (began to stretch and break wind), many with hangovers.
They soon reenter the cottage where the newly married couple
are still abed, and lay their simple wedding gifts on the coverlet.
Two of the local girls are given contrasting sketches: one is
lighthearted and "kanty" (happy), but *"Mause* begrutten [in
tears] was and bleer'd" because she had lost her virginity the
night before. One of the older women, Maggy, consoles her
with the thought that this is a common occurrence and not
the end of the world, with an amusingly worded example from
her own experience (stanza 9):

Or Bairns can read, they first	*before children;*
maun spell,	*must*
I learn'd this frae my Mammy,	*from*
And coost a Legen-girth my sell,	*cast* (*lost*); *lower hoop*
Lang or I married *Tammie.*	*before*

Then the celebration begins all over again, even more wildly than on the previous day.

Ramsay is generally effective in portraying these scenes of drunkenness, horseplay, and bickering between husbands and wives. He manages the complex verse form skillfully throughout. But this last part of his "Christis Kirk" is not quite so strong or delightful as canto 2, mainly because of the labored effect of the folklore. In stanza 12, for example, we have the "creeling of the groom," a custom Ramsay has to explain in a footnote: "For Merryment, a Creel or Basket is bound, full of Stones, upon his Back; and if he has acted a manly Part, his young Wife with all imaginable Speed cuts the Cords, and relieves him from the Burthen. If she does not, he's rallied for a Fumbler." Similarly, in stanzas 16 and 17, he gives us "The Riding of the Stang on a Woman that hath beat her Husband," an even more elaborate ritual that is artistically obtrusive and boring. These episodes, self-conscious and strained, detract from canto 3, but do not nullify its effectiveness otherwise.

On the whole, Ramsay's continuations of "Christis Kirk on the Green" are a notable achievement, a sustained effort of rollicking action, humorous caricature, and realistic dialogue that is mainly successful. He cleverly bridges the gap from the old poem, and he catches much of its spirit and flavor—though not its wild comic momentum. In doing this, and in doing it so well, Ramsay gave a vital new impetus to the "Christis Kirk" tradition; he showed its adaptability to modern times, and he paved the way for the more brilliant exploitation of the form by Fergusson and Burns. His cantos are no small achievement.

Ramsay's only other poem in the "Christis Kirk" form is dated May 1720, "Edinburgh's Salutation to the Most Honourable, My Lord Marquess of Carnarvon" (*STS*, 1:149–51), consisting of six stanzas in a kind of Scoto-English style—that is, the language is basically standard English with a thin sprinkling of Scots words or spellings. This is a fairly competent effort, though the personification of Edinburgh welcoming a distinguished visitor is somewhat strained, and the piece as a whole comes nowhere near the spriteliness and vigor of Ramsay's earlier cantos.

"A Tale of Three Bonnets"

This dramatic poem (*STS*, 3:7–31) in four cantos and 669 lines is Ramsay's longest original work in Scots or English, apart from *The Gentle Shepherd*. Like Ramsay's continuations of "Christis Kirk," it has suffered from unaccountable neglect at the hands of the critics. Woodhouselee, himself an ardent Unionist, did not appreciate Ramsay's strong anti-Unionist views (which he calls "absurd") in this work; as a result he devotes to it only a sentence or two of faint praise as a work of art.[7] Of recent critics, Martin, Daiches, and Lindsay ignore the poem altogether, while Kinghorn (*STS*, 4:15) barely mentions it, and that only in connection with Ramsay's political ideas. Surely, as Ramsay's second longest work the tale deserves some discussion—and it has more positive merits, as we shall see.

The date of "A Tale of Three Bonnets" is problematic, but it is generally thought to be an early work that Ramsay did not dare to publish until 1722, and then only as an anonymous pamphlet. It did not appear among his official collected works until 1729. Most probably Ramsay composed the tale for the amusement of his radical friends in the Easy Club; if so, the year 1715 will have to suffice as an educated guess. In any event, this dramatic poem is a hard-hitting political satire on the Act of Union, in the form of transparent allegory that would have been instantly clear to all of Ramsay's readers. In form the work is a series of dramatic dialogues among various characters, enclosed within a narrative framework spoken by "Bard" (Ramsay himself). The framework arrangement anticipates the structure of Ramsay's *The Gentle Shepherd,* where each scene is introduced by a chatty, colloquial prologue. For his verse form Ramsay employs another traditional Scots meter, the tetrameter couplet.

The characters in "A Tale of Three Bonnets" are listed at the beginning, with descriptive phrases, and their allegorical significances become quickly apparent. Following "Bard" we have "Duniwhistle, *Father* to Bristle, Joukum, *and* Bawsy," who represents the old historic independence of Scotland. "Bristle, *A Man of Honour and Resolution"* is clearly the contemporary, independent, patriotic son of Scotland of the type of Andrew

Fletcher of Saltoun who led the fight against the parliamentary
Union of Scotland and England. Next comes "Joukum, *In love
with Rosie,*" the Anglophile Scot seduced by "English gold";
followed by "Bawsy, *A Weak Brother*" whose epithet is self-
explanatory. "Rosie, *An Heiress*" is obviously the red rose of
England, loaded with wealth. Finally, there is "Ghost, *Of* Duniwhistle," and, amusingly, "Beef, *Porter to Rosie.*"

In the opening canto Duniwhistle, on his deathbed, bequeaths
to his sons the three bonnets which represent the ancient vir-
tues and integrity of Scotland, a proud heritage that has been
handed on from generation to generation for many centuries.
He admonishes them (*STS,* 3:8) never to surrender their birth-
right:

> And if ye'd hae nae Man betray ye,   *have no*
> Let naithing ever wile them frae ye,   *nothing; steal*
> But keep the BONNETS on your Heads,
> And Hands frae signing foolish Deeds.

All three sons swear never to give up their bonnets. "Bard"
then intrudes to tell us that Duniwhistle was scarcely in his
grave before the promise was broken by two of the sons (Joukum and Bawsy) as a consequence of Joukam's falling in love
with the flamboyant Rosie. The description of Rosie who lives,
of course, south of the border hills, is especially entertaining,
including two lines ("She was a winsome Wench and waly, /
And cou'd put on her Claiths fu' brawly") that were to stick
in the memory of Burns and to affect a famous passage in "Tam
O'Shanter" ("But *Tam* kend what was what fu' brawlie, / There
was ae winsome wench and wawlie").[8] The remainder of canto
1 is taken up with Joukum's crass wooing of Rosie—a strong
satiric scene in which the mercenary motives of both characters
are stressed. Rosie finally agrees to marry Joukum on condition
that he break his father's will and turn over to her the three
bonnets of Scotland.

In canto 2 Joukum approaches Bristle with promises of riches
if he will give up his ancestral bonnet. Bristle explodes in righ-
teous anger at the suggestion of this base deal, and attacks Joukum (*STS,* 3:17) in a passage of cutting vigor:

Thou vile Disgrace of our Forbeers,	*forebears*
Wha lang with valiant Dint of Weirs,	*long; blow; wars*
Maintain'd their Rights 'gainst a' Intrusions	
Of our auld Faes the	*old foes;*
Rosycrucians,	*English (red cross)*
Do'st thou design at last to catch	
Us in a Girn with this base Match,	*snare*
And for the hading up thy Pride,	*holding up*
Upon thy Breether's Riggings ride?	*brother's back*
I'll see you hang'd and her thegither. . . .	*together*

This is followed in canto 3 by Joukum's approach to the slovenly Bawsy, whom he easily bribes into giving up his bonnet. In this section the Bard's extended description of Bawsy's filthy cottage is particularly rich in comic realism.

In canto 4 Joukum delivers two of the three bonnets to Rosie. They are interrupted by the "Ghaist" (ghost) of Duniwhistle who denounces them both and so frightens Joukum that Rosie has to "soup him up with Usquebae" (whisky) to revive his courage. The marriage of Joukum and Rosie then takes place, with the understanding that Rosie will now have a free hand with the resources of Scotland. It should be noted that Rosie gets two out of the three bonnets, a proportion that roughly corresponds to the actual vote in the Scottish parliament in 1707 in favor of the Union.

In the last part of Ramsay's allegory the disastrous results of the marriage are shown. Rosie and Joukum squander Rosie's wealth until they are deeply in debt and Rosie must send Joukum back to *"Fairyland,"* that is, Scotland, to raise rents and taxes a mere thirty percent to support their high living. Ramsay's satire here (*STS, 3:26*) is devastating:

Away, with strict Command, he's sent	
To *Fairyland* to lift the Rent,	*Scotland*
And with him mony a *Catterpillar*	
To rug from *Birss* and *Bawsy* Siller;	*drag; Bristle; silver*
For her braid Table maun be serv'd,	*broad; must*
Tho' Fairy-fowk shou'd a' be starved.	*i.e., the Scots*

Bristle is furious, but legally helpless; Bawsy, greedily expecting riches, is treated with contempt and ridicule by Beef (Rosie's flunky) and is easily placated with false promises from Rosie and Joukum. And thus the seduction and humiliation of Scotland is accomplished.

Though "A Tale of Three Bonnets" is seldom brilliant in style, it is consistently well written, with a few passages of "hamely" colloquial imagery that are very effective. This dramatic poem is a daring, patriotic attack upon the Union which Ramsay depicts as a shameful surrender of independence for supposed economic benefits that prove to be illusory. Bawsy, for instance, is forced to pay for the extravagances of Rosie and Joukum, and is despised by them in the bargain. Like most of his countrymen Ramsay mistrusted the Union; he was indeed passionately opposed to it, and in this tale he frankly says so. That does not mean that Ramsay was a radical—politically, economically, or socially. On the contrary, he was fundamentally conservative, and leery of what seemed to him to be drastic and untrustworthy solutions such as the Union. His anti-Union sentiment is part of his special Scottish conservatism; he wished to preserve traditional Scottish values and the main thrust of his literary career is in that direction. He was prudent enough, however, to publish "A Tale of Three Bonnets" anonymously; there was no need to give offense to some of his powerful friends who happened to be on the other side of this issue. Nevertheless, "A Tale of Three Bonnets" is a courageous, outspoken, and quite remarkable satire that has been undervalued or totally ignored in Ramsay scholarship. It deserves to be recognized as one of his major works.

Comic Elegies

The Scots comic elegy tradition was inaugurated about 1640 by a talented Renfrewshire laird, Robert Sempill of Beltrees, in his celebrated poem "The Life and Death of Habbie Simson, the Piper of Kilbarchan," followed by a second elegy in the same style called "Epitaph on Sanny Briggs." For his verse form Sempill adopted a stanza that was fairly common in late medieval poetry in Scotland and northern England, consisting of six lines rhymed *a a a b a b,* with tetrameter lines for the *a* rhymes and dimeters for the *b*'s.[9] This stanza in the next century was christened "Standart Habby" by Allan Ramsay (*STS*, 1:119), became the favorite of both Fergusson and Burns, and in more recent times has often been called the "Burns stanza." The witty, clinching effect of the final rhyme makes it well suited for comic or satiric purposes, as the opening stanza of Sempill's "Habbie Simson" will show:

> Kilbarchan now may say alas!
> For she hath lost her game and grace,
> Both *Trixie* and *The Maiden Trace,*   (*bagpipe tunes*)
>   But what remead?   *remedy*
> For no man can supply his place:
>   Hab Simsons dead.[10]

Sempill's poem became the prototype of a new Scots satiric genre. In it the subject is usually an eccentric local character who has in fact died. The narrator expresses comically exaggerated grief as he describes the past life of the departed with good-natured satire, in such a way as to leave the final impression that the subject was a worthy person in spite of peculiarities, or because of them. "Habbie Simson" itself is by no means a great comic poem; though it has several flashes of genuine wit, on the whole it is no more than competent. Yet this poem, perhaps partly by virtue of its effective verse form, caught the popular imagination to such an extent that by Ramsay's time it was no doubt the most widely known and loved of Scots comic pieces. It was, therefore, inevitable that the young Ramsay should be drawn to this genre.

Altogether, Ramsay composed six comic elegies in the "Habbie" stanza; the four that he thought fit to publish—those on Maggy Johnston, John Cowper, Lucky Wood, and Patie Birnie—were all products of the first phase of his career. The dates of composition of some of these elegies are slightly uncertain.[11] The historical Maggy Johnston died in 1711, and there is evidence that Ramsay's elegy in some form existed in 1712, which makes it one of the very earliest of his surviving works. The poem on John Cowper is dated "Anno 1714" by Ramsay himself. Lucky Wood died in 1717, and Ramsay dated his poem in May of that year. All three of these early elegies were published together in pamphlet form in 1718. The one on Patie

Birnie was first published in 1720. Ramsay's last two elegies, unpublished during his lifetime, were certainly later. That on Magy Dickson, who was hanged in 1724, could not have been written earlier than that year; the final elegy, on Samuel Clerk, is wholly uncertain as to date but is probably still later.

"Elegy on Maggy Johnston, who died *Anno* 1711" (*STS*, 1:10–13) celebrates a famous alewife who kept a tavern on a small farm about a mile south of Edinburgh on the southern edge of the ancient golf course of Bruntsfield Links. Maggy was popular among all classes, Ramsay tells us, because of her low prices, genial disposition, and, above all, her "Pawky [cunning] Knack / Of brewing Ale amaist [almost] like Wine." Ramsay's poem is, of course, based solidly on the tradition established by Sempill's comic elegies, even to the extent that he echoes in his thirteenth stanza the "remead—dead" rhyme from "Habbie Simson." But Ramsay departs from his model in one significant respect: whereas Sempill's tributes to Habbie Simson and Sanny Briggs are taken up with amusing descriptions of those characters, Ramsay devotes only four of his fifteen stanzas to Maggy Johnston herself. The bulk of his elegy consists of fond reminiscences of happy times in Maggy's "Howff" (tavern), including hearty drinking parties, the playing of "Hyjinks" (a drunken game similar to the modern "chug-a-lug"), the enjoyment of tasty snacks, a personal account of falling into a drunken sleep in a nearby field on a summer night, and so forth. Stanza 4 is typical:

When in our Poutch we fand some Clinks,	*pocket; coins*
And took a Turn o'er *Bruntsfield-Links,*	
Aften in *Maggy's* at Hy-jinks,	
We guzl'd Scuds,	*ale*
Till we cou'd scarce wi hale out Drinks	*wholly downed*
Cast aff our Duds.	*clothes*

The poem is full of this kind of youthful bravado; its real subject is conviviality, Ramsay and his friends having fun at Maggy's, rather than Maggy herself.

Ramsay's "Elegy on Maggy Johnston" is one of the most frequently anthologized of all his poems, but it is far from his best. As we have seen, it is one of his very earliest writings,

and it suffers from immaturity in substance and in technique.
Now and then there is a flash of wit or an effective trick rhyme,
as in the tenth stanza:

> Syne down on a green Bawk, I trow   *bank*
>   I took a Nap,
> And soucht a' Night Balillilow   *snored*
>   As sound's a Tap.   *top*

Such imaginative touches, however, are rare in "Maggy Johnston." On the whole, it is competent in style, but lacking in
subtlety and spark; it is a promising but relatively crude specimen
of Ramsay's earliest verse in Scots.

His next effort in this genre, "Elegy on John Cowper Kirk-
Treasurer's Man, Anno 1714" (*STS*, 1:14–17), is much better
and is historically very important. Ramsay's long prefatory note
to this poem defining for the benefit of "Strangers" the functions
of the Kirk-Treasurer and his man is interesting evidence that
even at this early stage in his career he hoped to interest readers
beyond the borders of Scotland. Obviously, for Scottish readers
this kind of information would have been wholly unnecessary;
from the beginning Ramsay was aiming at London as well as
at Edinburgh. He explains that in each town a Kirk-Treasurer
is appointed each year to oversee the private morals of the
parishioners, especially in matters of fornication and prostitution.
"The Treasurer being changed every Year, never comes to be
perfectly acquainted with the Affair; but their general Servant
continuing for a long Time, is more expert at discovering such
Persons, and the Places of their Resort, which makes him capable
to do himself and Customers both a good or an ill Turn. *John
Cowper* maintain'd this Post with Activity and good Success for
several Years."

Ramsay begins with a powerful stanza expressing mock grief:

> I wairn ye 'a to greet and drone,   *warn; weep*
> *John Cowper's* dead, Ohon! Ohon!   *Alas!*
> To fill his Post, alake there's none,   *alack*
>   That with sic Speed   *such*
> Cou'd sa'r Sculdudry out like *John*,   *smell whoring out*
>   But now he's dead.

Two things should be noted about this remarkable opening of a remarkable poem. For one thing, Ramsay deviates sharply from the typical comic elegy pattern by lamenting the death of a wholly unworthy, if not despicable, character—a slimy informer and extortionist of the type of Chaucer's Summoner, not at all comparable to the genial and entertaining figures of Habbie Simson, Sanny Briggs, or Maggy Johnston. Secondly, the narrator *seems* to approve of John Cowper. Though his point of view is slightly ambiguous, the speaker consistently praises Cowper as an efficient enforcer of kirk discipline. He deplores the passing of this hypocritical officer as a disaster for the municipality—"The Loss of him is publick Skaith" (injury)—and in stanza 6, he curses Death as the malevolent instrument of Edinburgh's deprivation:

> Fy upon Death, he was to blame
> To whirle poor *John* to his lang Hame;   *long home*
> But tho' his Arse be cauld, yet Fame,   *cold*
>   Wi' Tout of Trumpet,[12]
> Shall tell how *Cowper's* awfou Name   *awful*
>   Cou'd flie a Strumpet.   *frighten*

The voice here, and throughout, is surely not Ramsay's, but rather that of a bigoted prude, one of Edinburgh's evangelical Calvinists.

In short, Ramsay's method in this elegy is that of lively burlesque, an important and daring innovation in the "Habbie" tradition. He adopts the voice of the "enemy" in order to make his point of view as ludicrous and loathsome as possible in his grief for the reprobate Cowper. As John C. Weston has pointed out in a very perceptive essay,[13] Ramsay's use of the ironic voice in this poem provided a crucial hint for Burns's brilliant exploitation of the burlesque technique in such poems as "The Holy Tulzie," "The Ordination," and "Holy Willie's Prayer." Further, Ramsay's addition of a witty "Postscript" to the elegy may have suggested to Burns the same device in "Tam Samson's Elegy" and "Epistle to William Simson."

On the whole, the "Elegy of John Cowper" is the most original and historically important of Ramsay's comic elegies. Artistically, it is far superior in technique and imagination to the one on Maggy Johnston. It is also one of the most underrated of his Scots poems.

Ramsay's third effort in this genre, "Elegy on Lucky Wood in the Canongate, May 1717" (*STS*, 1:18–21), is, like his poem on Maggie Johnston, a celebration of a local tavern keeper, but this time with the more traditional emphasis on the character of the woman herself. In Ramsay's day the Canongate (now part of central Edinburgh) was a separate municipality, a suburb of the city extending from the Nether-bow Port, the city gate at the eastern end of the High Street, down the slope to the palace of Holyroodhouse. The elegy contains several allusions to local matters which Ramsay has to explain in footnotes, including an amusing reference to Aikenhead (stanza 10), the porter at the Nether-bow who customarily locked up the city gate at midnight. Late drinkers at Lucky Wood's, like Ramsay and his friends, returning in the wee hours of the morning, would have to bribe Aikenhead with gills of whisky to open the gate and let them back into the city.

Ramsay opens his elegy with the usual expressions of comically exaggerated grief, including the notable second stanza:

> Hear me ye Hills, and every Glen,
> Ilk Craig, ilk Cleugh, and hollow Den,   *every rock; cleft*
> And Echo shrill, that a' may ken   *know*
>   The waefou Thud,   *woeful blow*
> Be rackless Death, wha came unsenn   *by reckless; unsent for*
>   To Lucky Wood.

This strong and witty stanza must have impressed Burns, since echoes of it crop up in phrases and in the overall conception of his "Elegy on Captain Matthew Henderson."[14] Most of Ramsay's elegy, however, is taken up with spritely and humorous praise of Lucky Wood's general excellence and neatness as an alewife, and especially of her generosity with free food. Stanza 7 is typical:

> She had the Gate sae weel to please,   *way so well*
> With *gratis* Beef, dry Fish, or Cheese;
> Which kept our Purses ay at Ease,   *always*
>   And Health in Tift,   *good order*
> And lent her fresh Nine Gallon Trees   *barrels*
>   A hearty Lift.

The final "Epitaph" on Lucky Wood also anticipates the endings of Burns's elegies on Henderson and on Tam Samson.[15] Moreover, the entire poem was destined to influence Robert Fergusson's sparkling description of Lucky Middlemist's oyster cellar in "Caller Oysters."[16]

As a whole, the "Elegy on Lucky Wood" is a skillful and delightful poem. It gives us a genial satiric view of night life in old Edinburgh, with the emphasis on the lighthearted and more wholesome aspects of that world, with nothing of the crudity or immaturity of "Maggy Johnston." Though it lacks the imaginative boldness of "John Cowper," it is at least its equal in craftsmanship, and it shows Ramsay steadily increasing in stylistic control as a comic poet in vernacular Scots.

"The Life and Acts of, or An Elegy on Patie Birnie" (*STS,* 1:186–91), composed about 1720, is the longest (twenty-one stanzas) of Ramsay's comic elegies and the last of them that he chose to publish; it is also, at least in terms of style and craftsmanship, the most accomplished. Here, even more than in "Lucky Wood," Ramsay follows the pattern of Sempill's "Habbie Simson" very closely, partly because his subject, a famous fiddler of Kinghorn (on the coast of Fife across from Edinburgh), is a similar sort of eccentric local musician as the immortal Habbie. But Ramsay's elegy is by no means a servile imitation; it is wholly original in its details and is, in fact, a much superior poem when compared to Sempill's. As might be expected, "Patie Birnie" strongly influenced Burns in at least two respects, as we shall see.

After the usual amusing expressions of grief, Ramsay plunges into a series of anecdotes of the career and character of Patie Birnie. Though it takes some annotation by Ramsay to make several of Birnie's escapades clear, on the whole they are highly entertaining. In stanzas 3 to 5, for example, we see Birnie's standard trick to gain employment as a fiddler: whenever he saw wealthy looking strangers enter an inn he would rush breathlessly up to them, pretend that he had been sent for, apologize for being late, whip out his fiddle, and immediately start playing, with all kinds of ingratiating lies and hilarious antics—all expressed in a rich, colloquial Scots, with touches of burlesque.

In stanza 8 we learn that Patie began as a fiddler with a

home-made instrument with strings attached to a mare's skull.
Ramsay then draws a whimsical analogy from Greek mythology:

Sae some auld-gabet Poets tell,	*old-fashioned*
Jove's nimble Son and Leckie snell	*lackey sharp*
Made the first Fiddle of a Shell,	
On which *Apollo*,	
With meikle Pleasure play'd himsel	*great*
Baith Jig and Solo.	*both*

This clever stanza obviously suggested Burns's passage on another fiddler in "The Jolly Beggars":

> The wee Apollo
> Set off wi' ALLEGRETTO glee
> His GIGA SOLO—[17]

Ramsay next introduces (stanza 10) Birnie's pal "Jonny Stocks," identified in a footnote as "A Man of a low Stature, but very broad, a loving Friend of his, who used to dance to his Musick":

O *Jonny Stocks* what comes o' thee,	
I'm sure thou'lt break thy Heart and die;	
Thy *Birnie* gane, thou'lt never be	*gone*
Nor blyth nor able	
To shake thy short Houghs merrily	*thighs*
Upon a Table.	

And in the following stanza Ramsay's ludicrous picture of Jonny dancing with a much taller girl ("With Nose forgainst a Lass's Midle") gave yet another hint to Burns for his brilliantly farcical sketch in 'The Jolly Beggars" of the tiny fiddler smitten with love for the huge female pickpocket—"Her strappan limb an' gausy middle, / (He reach'd nae higher)." Similarly, Ramsay's surprise ending for the elegy in which he tells his readers to wipe away their tears because Patie Birnie, after all, is still alive ("He is not dead"), became the model for Burns's final stanza in "Tam Samson's Elegy" where the same kind of reversal is effected (*"Tam Samson's livin!"*).[18]

Of the several escapades in Birnie's career that Ramsay recalls
in this poem perhaps the most entertaining is the final one (stanzas 19 and 20). Here Ramsay explains that Patie went to the
battle of Bothwell-Brig in 1679, but decided, Falstaff-like, that
discretion was the better part of valor; he saw no point in risking
injury to his eyesight or to his precious "Fidle-Hand":

Right pawkily he left the Plain	*craftily*
Nor o'er his Shoulder look'd again,	
But scour'd o'er Moss and Moor amain,	*ran*
To Riecky straight,	*Reekie (Edinburgh)*
And tald how mony Whigs were slain	*told*
Before they faught.	*fought*

The smooth technique and wry wit of these lines are typical
of the poem as a whole. Incidentally, the "straight-faught"
rhyme in this stanza is an interesting illustration of the kind
of compromise with standard English spelling that Ramsay felt
obliged to make in his Scots poems, a pattern that was to be
followed by both Fergusson and Burns later in the century.
In those poems that he left unpublished during his lifetime Ramsay tended to use a more or less phonetic spelling, as we shall
see, a spelling that tried to approximate the actual sounds of
Scots speech in his day. But in the Scots poems that he revised
for publication Ramsay adopted, somewhat inconsistently, a sort
of semi-Anglicized spelling in order to make his work more
easily accessible to non-Scots readers. In his "Preface" to *Poems,
1721* (*STS*, 1:xviii–xx), he derides those pedants who "are ignorant of the Beauties of their Mother Tongue," defends his use
of Scots, argues that Scots blended with English provides richer
vocabulary and sound effects, and states that even his poems
in standard English are meant to be read with a Scots pronunciation. The Scots pronunciation of the word "straight" in this
instance would be "straught," providing an identical rhyme with
"faught" in the last line. Why, then, would Ramsay use the
English spelling for the one word and the Scots for the other?
He probably feared the "straught" might present a problem
for English readers, whereas "faught" would be clear enough
to all. Nevertheless, the inconsistency creates a slightly confused
effect, an effect that Ramsay must have felt was the lesser of

two evils, preferable to making himself incomprehensible to members of that wider audience that he hoped to interest.

In any event, the "Elegy on Patie Birnie" is a remarkably good poem, lively in its humor, consistently skillful in its style. It is not only his longest comic elegy, but also, artistically speaking, his best.

Ramsay's last two efforts in this genre are much less substantial and may be treated briefly. In 1724 he produced "Magy Dickson" (*STS*, 3:182–84), a rather slapdash poem in the comic elegy tradition, inspired by the incredible adventure of a local character who became an Edinburgh celebrity as "half-hangit Maggie Dickson." Kinghorn and Law in their note on this poem (*STS*, 6:132) summarize the whole affair neatly and eloquently: "In 1724, Margaret Dickson of Fisherrow, Musselburgh [a fishing village near Edinburgh], who had been separated from her husband for ten months, was hanged for concealing the birth of an illegitimate child. Cut down from the gallows, she recovered as she was being taken home for burial, and was none the worse for the experience except, as the *Caledonian Mercury* felicitously expressed it, for a pain in the neck." Ramsay's opening stanza will suffice to illustrate the quality as well as the phonetic spelling of this unpublished piece:

Assist ye Creil wives ane & a'	*creel (fish basket)*
of Musselbrugh & fisher Raw	
in souching sang the sooth to shaw	*breathing; show*
of that slee wife	*sly*
that after she was hangit staw	*stole*
again to Life.	

On the whole, "Magy Dickson" is a rather careless occasional poem, mildly amusing but seldom more than competent in style. The actual facts of this grotesque case are, indeed, funnier than Ramsay's poem about them; so that his mock elegy can hardly be called an artistic success.

"An Elegy on Mr. Samuel Clerk Running Stationer" (*STS*, 3:301–3), also unpublished by Ramsay and of uncertain date, is much better. Clerk was another local Edinburgh character, a "running stationer"—that is, a street vendor of books and pamphlets with no fixed place of business, or, as Ramsay puts it (stanza 3), "A Stationer without a Station." In this lively poem Ramsay focuses on three aspects of Clerk's character, beginning with his usefulness and courage as an impartial seller of controversial and sometimes treasonous political pamphlets (stanzas 3–5). Then we learn (stanzas 4–6) that his parents had intended him for a career in the ministry, "But his wise Head— / To Arts mair usefou was inclined." Ramsay wryly explains in stanza 5 that Clerk was ill suited to the ecclesiastical life because his tender soul could not stand the petty bickering of theological disputes:

His Saul sublimer could na bear,	*soul*
The Sturt, the Struggle, strife, and Steer,	*strife; stir*
Hair-cleaving, *grano-salis* weir,	*hair-splitting;*
About the Creed;	*grain-of-salt war*
And calling ane annither Liar,	
But now he's Dead.	

This is witty enough, but even more entertaining is the last part of the elegy (stanzas 8–13) on Clerk's addiction to strong drink ("Delicious Drams were his Delight") and on his rumored liaison with his hard-drinking landlady (stanza 11):

What else he acted with this Lady,	
The Muse say'th not, tho some are ready,	
To swear he try'd to be a Dady,	*daddy (father)*
But came nae speed;	*got nowhere*
He being not o'er stout or steady,	
For sic a Deed.	*such*

The elegy on Samuel Clerk is a relatively polished performance, in contrast to "Magy Dickson," with more or less orthodox spelling and capitalization, a fact which leads us to suspect that Ramsay prepared it for publication but never got round to it, or changed his mind for some reason. However that may be, it is a charming piece of good-natured wit, well worth reading.

Ramsay's comic elegies, taken together, are a significant achievement. Starting with a very popular seventeenth-century poem, Sempill's "Habbie Simson," as his inspiration, Ramsay developed the form far beyond the limitations of his model.

In "John Cowper" he introduced a burlesque method wholly new to this genre, as well as a sharper edge of satire. In "Patie Birnie" and to a lesser extent in "Lucky Wood" and "Samuel Clerk" he surpassed Sempill in general wittiness and sophistication of style. Looked at chronologically, Ramsay's elegies show a steady improvement (except for the sloppy "Magy Dickson") from the relative awkwardness of "Maggie Johnston" to the smooth and skillful effects of the later pieces. For the eighteenth-century Scots revival Ramsay himself, in fact, *created* the comic elegy as an important genre which he passed on to Fergusson and Burns.

Mock Testaments and Other Satiric Genres

Ramsay's Scots satires include two notable specimens of the "mock testament" or "last dying words" type. This genre has medieval roots, but Ramsay's immediate model was undoubtedly Hamilton of Gilbertfield's "Last Dying Words of Bonny Heck"[19] which he found in Watson's *Choice Collection.* For this poem Hamilton used the "Habbie" stanza and also the beast fable method; his speaker is a dog, "A Famous Greyhound in the Shire of Fife," so that his "Bonny Heck" provided the obvious precedent for Burns's "The Death and Dying Words of Puir Mailie" where the speaker is a sheep.[20] For his own purposes Ramsay omitted the animal speaker, but adopted the verse form and "last dying words" device of Hamilton's work.

Ramsay's earliest effort in this genre is "Lucky Spence's Last Advice" (*STS,* 1:22–26), apparently composed in 1718. Lucky Spence was another well-known Edinburgh character, the keeper of a brothel near the palace of Holyroodhouse. In an opening stanza of narrative Ramsay depicts the old bawd, about to expire, calling her team of young whores to her bedside to hear her final admonitions; the rest of the poem, sixteen "Habbie" stanzas, presents her dying words. The second and third stanzas typify the flavor of the whole:

My loving Lasses, I maun leave ye,	*must*
But dinna wi' ye'r Greeting grieve me,	*weeping*
Nor wi' your Draunts and Droning	*sighs*
deave me,	*deafen*

But bring's a Gill;	*glass of whisky*
For Faith, my Bairns, ye may believe me,	*children*
'Tis 'gainst my Will.	

O Black Ey'd *Bess* and mim Mou'd *Meg,*	*modest mouthed*
O'er good to work or yet to beg;	
Lay Sunkots up for a sair Leg,	*something; sore*
For whan ye fail,	
Ye'r Face will not be worth a Feg,	*fig*
Nor yet ye'r Tail.	

This is fairly spirited stuff; the poet exploits his verse form with skill, making deft satiric use of the end-rhymes in each stanza. Ramsay portrays the way of life of the prostitute with relentless realism, stressing the appalling risks of disease and imprisonment as well as the cash rewards that result from utterly unscrupulous methods. In stanza 6, for example, Lucky Spence gives sage advice on rolling a helpless drunk:

Cleek a' ye can be Hook or Crook,	*grab*
Ryp ilky Poutch frae Nook to Nook;	*every pocket*
Be sure to truff his Pocket-book,	*steal*
Saxty Pounds *Scots*	*sixty*
Is nae deaf Nits: in little bouk	*empty nuts (worthless); bulk*
Lie great Bank-Notes.	

"Lucky Spence," in general, affords vivid pictures of low life in Ramsay's Edinburgh. It is moderately successful as a comic treatment of the oldest profession, presenting glimpses of squalid human degradation in a way that makes us laugh rather than cry—with humor and some lively wit. Artistically, this is fairly effective comic poetry, though not among Ramsay's very best pieces.

Ramsay's other effort in this genre, "The Last Speech of a Wretched Miser" (*STS,* 2:62–68), is more impressive. First published in 1724 and probably written in that year, this poem is notable in at least three respects. For one thing, it is Ramsay's most sustained work in the "Habbie" verse form, with twenty-nine stanzas and 174 lines. Secondly, it differs from most of Ramsay's Scots satires in that it appears to be a generalized attack upon a human type rather than a personal satire on an individual—though, of course, the poet may have had one or more actual men in mind.[21] Finally, and somewhat surprisingly, it is a remarkably good poem, a piece of comic grotesquerie, full of extravagantly earthy but effective images that make it one of Ramsay's most imaginative works.

Ramsay's "Miser" is totally unrepentant; in his dying words he simply explains and graphically illustrates his obsession, and his only regret is that he cannot take his money with him but must leave it to a spendthrift son. He compares his long, painful struggle to amass wealth to that of Tantalus ("Chin deep into a Siller Flood"), or to the self-denying vigilance of eunuchs guarding Oriental harems (stanza 4):

> Or like the wissen'd beardless Wights,   *dried out; men*
> Wha herd the Wives of Eastern Knights,
> Yet ne'er enjoy the saft Delights
>   Of Lasses bony;
> Thus did I watch lang Days and Nights
>   My lovely Money.

After this brilliant analogy the Miser goes on to detail the incredible economies to which he gladly subjected himself. He tells us in the seventh stanza that "I never wore my Claiths [clothes] with brushing, / Nor wrung away my Sarks [shirts] with washing," and in the ninth—

> Nor kept I servants, Tales to tell,
> But toom'd my Coodies a' my sell;   *emptied; chamber pots*
> To hane in Candle I had a Spell   *save; trick*
>   Baith cheap and bright,   *both*
> A Fish-head, when it 'gins to smell,
>   Gives curious Light.

There are several passages in the poem as telling as these, but one more must suffice to demonstrate its power. Toward the end of his speech (stanza 24) the Miser sums up the terrible sacrifices he has made:

O Gear! I held ye lang thegither	*property; together*
For you I starv'd my good auld Mither,	*old mother*
And to *Virginia* sald my Brither,	*sold*
And crush'd my Wife:	
But now I'm gawn I kenna whither;	*going; know not*
To leave my Life.	

All things considered, "The Last Speech of a Wretched Miser" is one of Ramsay's finest poems. Despite its generalized subject, it is full of bold, concrete images that give it a kind of imaginative force that is unusual in Ramsay's work. The unabashed confessional quality reminds one of Chaucer's *Pardoner's Prologue;* the speech's strong, gritty comedy is an impressive achievement, generally underrated by the critics.[22]

Two or three others of Ramsay's Scots satires deserve mention, including "The Rise and Fall of the Stocks, 1720" (*STS*, 1:176–82). This piece in tetrameter couplets is in the form of an epistle to Lord Ramsay, dated 25 March 1721, and is a moderately witty satire on foolish speculations on the South Sea Bubble. Ramsay uses as his motto four lines from Samuel Butler's *Hudibras* and his work is clearly modeled on that poem. The opening paragraph with its comic personification of the nation is especially spritely (lines 4–8):

Viewing our poor bambousl'd Nation,	
Biting her Nails, her Knuckles wringing,	
Her Cheek sae blae, her Lip sae hinging;	*blue; hanging*
Grief and Vexation's like to kill her,	
For tyning baith her Tick and Siller.	*losing; credit; cash*

Unfortunately, Ramsay fails to maintain this level of style through the 196 lines of his topical epistle. It is generally competent and mildly amusing, but lacks imaginative spark; Maurice Lindsay is correct in characterizing this piece as a kind of "versified journalism."[23]

"The Marrow Ballad" (*STS*, 3:244–45) is a very different story. This trenchant satire on religious bigotry, never published during Ramsay's lifetime, bears the subtitle "On Seeing a Strolling Congregation Going to a Field Meeting, May 9th, 1738," and is written to the tune of the popular seventeenth-century

song "Fy let us a' to the Bridal." In their notes to this poem
Kinghorn and Law (*STS,* 6:152) quietly assert that the "poem
has resemblances, in style and attitude, to Burns's *Holy Fair.*"
That is surely an understatement, since the resemblances are
quite astonishing, not only in style and attitude but also in the
structural method of highlighting the dramatic contrasts between
the pious preaching and the profane behavior of lads and lasses
in the congregation. The general resemblances are indeed so
striking that one would be tempted to see in Ramsay's poem
the catalyst for Burns's, were it not for the fact that it is improba-
ble in the extreme that Burns could ever have seen this poem
in manuscript.

In "The Marrow Ballad" Ramsay launches an ironic attack
upon the extreme Presbyterian position as represented by such
popular preachers as Erskine and Mair of the breakaway Associ-
ate Synod.[24] The opening lines set the tone very deftly:

> O fy let us a' to the meeting
> for there will be canting there
> Where some will be laughing some greeting   *weeping*
> at the preaching of Erskine and Mair.[25]

In his next stanzas Ramsay goes on to suggest, as Burns does
in "The Holy Fair," not only that these religious revival meet-
ings provide opportunities for boys and girls to get together
for lovemaking, but also that the mood of spiritual exaltation
induced by the sermons leads directly into sexual passion. Ramsay's speaker throughout is a young man on the way to the
field meeting (stanza 3):

> The sun will be sunk in the west
> before they have finished the wark   *work*
> then behind a whin Bush we can rest—   *gorse*
> ther's mekle good done in the dark.   *much*
> There Tammy to Tibby may creep
> Slee Sandy may mool in with Kate   *muzzle in (kiss)*
> while other dowf sauls are asleep   *dull souls*
> we'll handle deep matters of State.

Later, in the opening lines of the final stanza, the speaker gives
ironic thanks to the ministers for providing such ideal conditions

for love, and then slips in an incisive thrust at their rigid fanaticism:

> Then up with the Brethren true blew   *blue*
>   wha lead us to siccan delight   *who; such*
> and can prove it altho they be few
>   that ther is naebody els wha is right.

That last line, in its context, is wonderfully devastating.

Why did Ramsay leave this fine poem unpublished? Discreet as he was in this late stage of his career (1738), after he had made his fortune, Ramsay no doubt was reluctant to give offense; perhaps also he worried about libel suits, since the poem names the names of distinguished churchmen. In any case, he held it back, and "The Marrow Ballad" remained buried in an obscure manuscript for well over two centuries. It ranks high among his satires and deserves to be widely known.

Summary

Obviously, Ramsay's Scots satires constitute a major part of his significant poetry. One striking fact about them is that, with the exception of the "Christis Kirk" cantos, parts of "A Tale of Three Bonnets," and one or two others, all of these satires deal with town life—especially with Edinburgh, "Auld Reekie," the old greystone jungle of narrow wynds and closes flanking the High Street and Canongate, the crowded, battered, squalid, vibrant city he lived in all of his adult life and clearly loved. The vivid impressions of that unique world that we get in these poems look back two centuries to the incisive Edinburgh satires of William Dunbar, and they provided a solid modern precedent for the brilliant Edinburgh poems of Robert Fergusson fifty years later.

Another point worth noticing in these satires is that in them Ramsay limited himself to three verse forms: the "Christis Kirk" stanza, the "Habbie" stanza, and the tetrameter couplet—all traditional Scottish meters. The only exception to this, "The Marrow Ballad," is composed in a pattern very closely related both in form and spirit to the "Christis Kirk" tradition. In so doing Ramsay succeeded in showing that these ancient native poetic forms were still alive and adaptable to modern themes, and he passed them on, reinvigorated, to his successors. At the same time, he revealed the possibilities of the burlesque method for modern Scots satire in "John Cowper," "Lucky Spence," and "Wretched Miser"—a development that was to have a profound effect on Burns.

How good are Ramsay's Scots satires intrinsically? As we have seen, their quality is uneven, and we should not claim too much for them. "Maggy Johnston" is awkward and immature, "Magy Dickson" is sloppy, others are no more than competent. But in the best of them—including the second canto of "Christis Kirk," the bold experiment of "John Cowper," the skilled, genial satire of "Lucky Wood" and "Patie Birnie," the imaginative power of "Wretched Miser," and the cutting wit of "The Marrow Ballad"—Ramsay shows an impressive talent. Kinghorn, in the most recent and in many respects most valuable biographical and critical work on Ramsay (*STS*, 4:1–169), largely ignores these remarkable satires, preferring to focus on his pastoral poetry, adaptations of Horace, and editorial labors. But the Scots satires cannot be ignored; they belong to the vital, central part of Ramsay's life work.

Chapter Three

Scots Epistles and Odes

The works of the graceful Roman poet Horace—his epistles, odes, and satires—were very popular among the literati in eighteenth-century Scotland. Horace was a favorite in England too, and on the Continent as well, but for some reason the Scots were especially fond of him. The Scottish poets of this century, including Ramsay, Fergusson, and Burns, shared a kind of Horatian ideal—a dream of peaceful retirement from the bustle and corruption of the town, or (in Burns's case) from backbreaking labor on the farm, to a life of literary leisure in some delicious rural estate, relieved from the cruel necessity of making a living. Horace himself, with the help of wealthy patrons, had escaped from Rome to enjoy such a quiet life on his Sabine farm. Of the foremost Scots poets of our period only Ramsay succeeded in realizing this dream, at least to some extent; Fergusson and Burns died striving for it.

It was therefore inevitable that Ramsay should have been attracted to the favorite poetic genres of Quintus Horatius Flaccus. He already knew, of course, some of the imitations of Horace's epistles by English poets of his own era whom he greatly admired, such poems as Matthew Prior's ironic and colloquial "Epistle to Fleetwood Shephard" (1689).[1] His commitment to the verse epistle in Scots, however, came about in 1719 more or less fortuitously through the initiative of William Hamilton of Gilbertfield (a country estate near Glasgow), a gentleman who had already achieved the Horatian dream. At about the same time Ramsay began experimenting on his own with free adaptations of the odes of Horace. In both of these Horatian genres Ramsay produced important work, but he was especially prolific in the verse epistle, composing at least sixteen of them in Scots during his lifetime. Let us turn first to the epistles.

Epistles to William Hamilton of Gilbertfield

Hamilton of Gilbertfield had already acquired a modest reputation as an amateur poet with the publication of his "The Last
Dying Words of Bonny Heck" in Watson's *Choice Collection* a
few years before Ramsay arrived on the literary scene. By 1719,
however, Ramsay himself had earned growing recognition as
a new Scots poet through his publication of several pieces that
Hamilton had seen and admired. So it happened that on 26
June 1719, out of a blue sky, so to speak, Hamilton wrote his
first Horatian verse epistle to Allan Ramsay in Edinburgh, in
the Scottish "Habbie" stanza and in the Scots tongue. In so
doing, Hamilton in fact invented the Scots verse epistle, a genre
that was destined to flourish mightily throughout the century
and beyond. William Hamilton deserves full credit for this surprising initiative that eventually led to the superb epistles of
Burns.[2] Its immediate result was an exchange of seven verse
letters of this kind with Ramsay—three by Hamilton, four by
Ramsay—all written between June and December of 1719 (*STS*,
1:115–37).

Hamilton's opening missive—and we must remember that
he was writing to a man he had never met—is naturally full
of jocular flattery, beginning as follows:

O Fam'd and celebrated ALLAN!
Renowned Ramsay, canty Callan,   *happy fellow*
Ther's nowther Highlandman nor Lawlan, *neither; Lowland*
    In Poetrie,
But may as soon ding down *Tamtallan*   *beat; (a strong castle)*
    As match wi' thee.

He goes on to praise Ramsay's verse as comparable to that of
Ben Jonson or Dryden, expresses the hope that they may be
able to get together over a bottle in an Edinburgh tavern, and
ends with a trick subscription worked into the end-line of his
final "Habbie" stanza: "Yours—wanton *Willy.*" This poem set
the pattern for the verse epistle in eighteenth-century Scotland,
with its relaxed conversational tone and witty vernacular idiom.

Ramsay's answer to Hamilton's letter is written in the same

form and is dated "Edinburgh, July 10th, 1719" (*STS*, 1:118–
21). He praises Hamilton's poems, mentioning "Bonny Heck"
by name in stanzas 2 and 5, and also (stanza 6) his mastery of
the "Habbie" verse form:

May I be licket wi' a Bittle,	*wooden club*
Gin of your Numbers I think little:	*if*
Ye're never rugget, shan, nor kittle,	*silly; difficult*
But blyth and gabby,	*glib*
And hit the Spirit to a Title,	*tittle*
Of Standart *Habby*.	

In his final stanzas Ramsay says that the English have heaped
honors on their poets while the Scots have neglected their poetic
heritage—poets like Gavin Douglas, kings James I and V, who
were even better than the English and were famous throughout
Europe. In stanza 10 he reflects on this splendid past:

On the lear'd Days of *Gawn Dunkell*,[3]	*learned*
Our country then a Tale cou'd tell,	
Europe had nane mair snack and snell	*clever; sharp*
At Verse or Prose;	
Our Kings were Poets too themsell,	
Bauld and Jocose.	*bold*

There is a strong national bias here, of course, but Ramsay
was wholly sincere and dedicated in his effort to restore the
older Scottish poets to their rightful place of honor.

Ramsay's response to Hamilton is, on the whole, lively and
interesting. There are some weak spots (stanza 9, for example,
has an awkward enjambment with stanza 10), but Ramsay's first
Scots epistle in the "Habbie" stanza is generally well written,
entertaining work.

Hamilton's next letter, "Epistle II" (*STS*, 1:121–24), followed swiftly a few days later on 24 July. With seventeen stanzas
it is the lengthiest piece in this poetic correspondence, and it
is smoothly and expertly written.[4] As in his first epistle Hamilton
here butters Ramsay up with exaggerated praise in genial, joking
style—including his invention in stanza 8 of the nickname "honest *Allie*," a phrase that was to stick to Ramsay permanently.

Ramsay's reply (*STS*, 1:125–27), dated 4 August, opens with a highly imaginative passage: in the first stanza he tells Hamilton that his excessive praise will turn the head of his "Muse"; then, in the next three stanzas he presents, in brilliant burlesque, the Muse's outraged response to this idea. Stanza 2 is especially engaging:

SAID I,—"Whisht, quoth the vougy Jade,	*silence;* *proud bitch*
"*William*'s a wise judicious Lad,	
"Has Havins mair than e'er ye had, "Ill bred Bog-staker;	*good breeding* *-stalker*
"But me ye ne'er sae crouse had craw'd,	*without; happily;* *crowed*
"Ye poor Scull-thacker."	*-thatcher*

This is sparkling, farcical comedy, as Ramsay makes fun of his early menial occupations, having the "Muse" say that if it had not been for *her* he would still be herding sheep as a miserable "Bog-staker" in Leadhills, or making wigs as a "poor Scull-thacker" in Edinburgh. The rest of the epistle falls considerably below the lively wit of the first four stanzas, although Ramsay's ninth is neatly done:

Set out the burnt Side of your Shin,	(*walk proudly*)
For Pride in Poets is nae Sin,	
Glory's the Prize for which they rin,	*run*
And Fame's their Jo;	*sweetheart*
And wha blews best the Horn shall win;	*who blows*
And wharefore no?	*why not?*

Three weeks later, on 24 August, Hamilton answered with "Epistle III" (*STS*, 1:128–30). In his third stanza he pays a graceful and amusing tribute to Ramsay's "Lucky Spence":

Of thy last Poem, bearing Date	
August the Fourth, I grant Receipt;	
It was sae bra, gart me look blate,	*fine; made; shy*
'Maist tyne my Senses,	*almost lose*
And look just like poor Country *Kate*	
In Lucky *Spence*'s.	

After some skilled, lighthearted banter about Ramsay's "Muse" and his own, Hamilton closes with a warm request for blessings on his poetic friend. Ramsay's reply, "Answer III," is dated 2 September and is, on the whole, the best of these epistles (*STS*, 1:131–34). He congratulates Hamilton, who had been an army lieutenant, upon his wisdom in retiring early from warlike strife; Julius Caesar should have done the same (stanza 3):

That Bang'ster Billy *Caesar July*,	*roaring fellow*
Wha at Pharsalia wan the Tooly,	*battle*
Had better sped, had he mair hooly	*quietly, slowly*
Scamper'd thro Life,	
And 'midst his Glories sheath'd his Gooly,	*knife*
And kiss'd his Wife.	

The trick rhymes here are very effective, and the overall conception is funny.

If there was ever any doubt about the Horatian influence on these epistles it is dispelled by stanzas 6 and 7 where Ramsay gives us a loose paraphrase of Horace's *Odes,* book 1, ode 11. His rendering of Horace's *carpe diem* theme into colloquial Scots, beginning "Ne'er fash [worry] about your neist [next] Year's State," is surprisingly felicitous, and it undoubtedly inspired Fergusson's adaptation of this same ode of Horace half a century later.[5] The rest of Ramsay's third epistle to Hamilton is carefully and wittily crafted, with a clever tail-rhyme signature in the final stanza:

I ne'er wi' lang Tales fash my Head,	*bother myself*
But when I speak, I speak indeed;	
Wha ca's me droll,	*calls;*
but ony Feed,	*without any quarrel*
I'll own I am sae,	*so*
And while my Champers can chew Bread,	*teeth*
Yours—ALLAN RAMSAY	

Some three months after this fine epistle, in late December of 1719, Ramsay wrote yet another verse letter to Hamilton, entitled, "An Epistle to Lieutenant Hamilton On the receiving the Compliment of a Barrel of Loch-Fine Herrings from him" (*STS*, 1:135–37). This poem is in seven stanzas of a curious ten-line form that seems to be a sort of experimental expansion of "Standart *Habby.*"[6] The first two stanzas, a humorous description of the herrings, are quite good; but after that the poem degenerates as Ramsay launches into praise of a Royal Fisheries scheme, with singy-songy rhythm and strained rhymes—mainly doggerel, not worth quoting.

On the whole, however, the Hamilton-Ramsay epistles are an important development, and they still make pleasant reading. Together, they established the Horatian verse epistle in Scots as a popular and distinctive genre for the future. They showed that the Scots language, in skilled hands, was remarkably well adapted to the informal, colloquial effects of Horace's epistles; and in so doing Hamilton and Ramsay created an original form for modern Scottish poetry.

Other Scots Epistles, 1719–36

Ramsay's first letter to Hamilton of Gilbertfield was not his earliest attempt at the verse epistle in Scots. Six months earlier, in January of 1719, he had written "An Epistle to Mr. James Arbuckle of Belfast, A.M." (*STS,* 1:212–17) in Scots tetrameter couplets. It is an occasional piece, somewhat carelessly written, but witty in spots, with feminine rhymes for a light, whimsical effect. There are many trick rhymes in the 137 lines of this epistle, some of them fairly good, but in several places the piece is marred by tortured rhythms. The second half of the poem (lines 69–125) is notable as a specimen of humorous, and flattering, self-description, beginning with some interesting physical details:

> *Imprimis* then, for Tallness I
> Am five Foot and four Inches high:
> A Black-a-vic'd snod dapper Fallow,   *swarthy neat*
> Nor lean, nor overlaid wi' Tallow.   *fat*

Ramsay then goes on to say that he is a man of cheerful mind; he hates drunks and gluttons but likes drink and food in moderation; he is neither Whig nor Tory, nor Catholic, nor fanatical cultist, but a solid Christian who is shrewd and skillful at making money. The epistle has a certain charm, but it is a rather unpolished piece of work that Ramsay wisely buried toward the back of his first volume of *Poems* (1721), whereas he gave his epistles with Gilbertfield a place of prominence nearer the front.

Much less enjoyable is "To Josiah Burchet, Esq." (*STS,* 1:113–14), written in the same year (1719). Burchett was a prominent Englishman who served as secretary of the admiralty from 1698 to 1742. He had written a poem to Ramsay in English heroic couplets (*STS,* 1:112–13), complimenting him on his Scots pastoral of "Richy and Sandy." Ramsay replies in the same verse form, but in Scots, in an epistle full of self-congratulation; he wallows in Burchett's praise and even compares himself (we hope facetiously) to the great classic poets of antiquity (lines 20–24):

> Whence far I glowr to the Fag-end of Time,   *stare*
> And view the Warld delighted wi' my Rhime.
> That when the Pride of sprush new Words are laid,   *spruce*
> I like the *Classick* Authors shall be read.

As Ramsay himself confesses elsewhere, he was never a modest man!

In 1722, following the favorable reception of his first volume of *Poems,* Ramsay produced three more verse epistles. "To His Grace John Duke of Roxburgh" (*STS,* 3:160–64) is dated 20 April 1722 and was never published by Ramsay. A Scots epistle in the "Christis Kirk" stanza, this is a typical piece of personal flattery to a wealthy patron, asking for his help in obtaining a small pension or sinecure; but it shows Ramsay's earlier extensive experience with the "Christis Kirk" meter and is fairly well done. Slightly better is another private verse letter, unpublished until recently, "To Mr. Jo. Kerr of King's College, Aberdeen" (*STS,* 3:158–60). This is a pleasant epistle in the ballad stanza, responding to one of Kerr's in which Ramsay was taken to task for not mentioning the lasses of Don and Dee (Aberdeenshire) in his poem "Tartana" where he had praised the "nymphs" of southern Scottish rivers such as Clyde, Tweed, and Tay. Ramsay confesses the omission and makes whimsical amends to the northern lasses (stanza 11):

> Dear Donian Nymphs cease to Reflect
> My fault I frankly own
> have for a penetent respect
> wha canna bear your frown

Here, as we see, the poet uses a kind of genteel, Scoto-English style—that is, he writes in what is basically standard English with a light sprinkling of Scots words or spellings—but he manages it with some delicacy and wit. Very different in tone is "To Mr. William Starrat" (*STS*, 2:72–73), another epistle of the same year in lively, colloquial Scots. This one, in pentameter couplets, is a reply to a verse letter from Starrat, a mathematics teacher at Strabane in Ireland, praising Ramsay's poems. It is moderately successful and shows that Ramsay's reputation, even at this early stage, had extended beyond the boundaries of Scotland.

Among the very best of Ramsay's Scots epistles is a product, apparently, of 1724, his "Epistle To the Honourable Duncan Forbes, Lord Advocate" (*STS*, 2:24–27). This is written largely in an unusual six-line stanza that seems to be a modification of the "Habbie" meter, but with trimeter tail-lines and a rhyme scheme of *a a b c c b*—the same stanza that Burns was to use later in "Extemporare Verses on Dining with Lord Daer."[7] It includes, furthermore, an extraordinarily effective passage (stanzas 4–8) on the false pride of the nouveaux riches, beginning as follows:

How mony, your Reverse, unblest,	
Whase Minds gae wandring through a Mist,	
Proud as the Thief in Hell,	
Pretend, forsooth, they're gentle Fowk.	*folk*
'Cause Chance gi'es them of Gear the Yowk,	*property; yolk*
And better Cheils the Shell?	*fellows*
I've seen a We'an aft vex it sell,	*child often*
And Greet, because it was not tall;	*weep*
Heez'd on a Board, O than!	*lifted*
Rejoicing in the artfu' Height,	
How smirky look'd the little Wight!	*fellow*
And thought it sell a Man.	

Sic Bairns are some blawn up a wee	*children; blown*
With Splendor, Wealth and Quality.	
Upon these Stilts grown vain;	
They o'er the Pows of poor Fowk stride. . . .	*heads; folk*

This passage and the epistle as a whole is strikingly Burnsian in theme and attitude. Ramsay boldly expresses his sense of the unfairness of an economic system that by the accident ("Chance") of inheritance raises fools above men of greater merit, a view that Burns was to give utterance to with even greater force and passion in "Song—For a' that and a' that," "Epistle to Davie," and many other poems.[8] Specifically, Ramsay's lines (59–60) "When struting [strutting] Nathings are despis'd / With a' their stinkan Pride" probably suggested the strutting image in the third stanza of Burns's "Song" as well as "their cursed pride" in his verse letter to Davie (line 14). Beyond that, Ramsay's laudatory stanzas (2–3, 9–10) on the Lord Advocate, in their self-conscious and somewhat ambiguous point of view, bear a general similarity to Burns's poem on "Lord Daer."

In the latter part of this epistle (lines 67–107) Ramsay inserts a rendering of a French fable by LaMotte[9] into Scots tetrameter couplets to illustrate his theme of false pride. He introduces this fable of the "Two Books" with a stanza of engaging wit:

This to set aff as I am able,	
I'll frae a *Frenchman* thigg a Fable,	*steal*
And busk it in a Plaid;	*dress*
And tho' it be a Bairn of *Motte*'s,	*child*
When I have taught it to speak *Scots,*	
I am its second Dad.	

The fable itself is a vituperative exchange between a book of trivial content in an expensive Turkish leather binding and a valuable work in an ordinary, worn cover. Ramsay's Scots version of this dialogue probably gave Robert Fergusson the idea for the new Scots poetic form, the "flyting [scolding] eclogue," that he created in such poems as "A Drink Eclogue," "The Mutual Complaint of Plainstanes and Causey," and "The

Ghaists," a form which Burns inherited in turn and used in "The Brigs of Ayr" and other poems.[10] Both Fergusson and Burns, then, must have known this epistle thoroughly and valued it highly—and rightly so. The "Epistle to Forbes" is vigorous and effective throughout, with smooth, accomplished style and some imaginative force; it shows Ramsay at his skillful best.

At about the same time (1724) Ramsay wrote an "Epistle to Robert Yarde of Devonshire, Esquire" (*STS,* 2:57–61). This verse letter is fairly long, in 142 lines of tetrameter couplets, but is rather undistinguished; it is a good, capable poem that lacks spark. In content this epistle is a set of obvious, orthodox moralities of the sort one finds in Burns's "Epistle to a Young Friend."[11] Its most entertaining passage comes in the opening paragraph, where Ramsay depicts with graphic humor the false stereotype of Scotland as a land of freezing deprivation (lines 5–10):

What sprightly tale in Verse can *Yarde*	
Expect frae a cauld *Scottish* Bard,	*cold*
With Brose and Bannocks poorly fed,	*broth; oat cakes*
In Hoden Gray right hashly cled,	*homespun; slovenly*
Skelping o'er frozen Hags with Pingle,	*running; bogs; pain*
Picking up Peets to beet his Ingle. . . .	*kindle; fire*

This is good fun, but the rest of "Epistle to Yarde" is less than memorable.

In 1727 appeared "To my kind and worthy Friends in Ireland, who on a Report of my Death, made and published several Elegies Lyrick and Pastoral, very much to my Honour" (*STS,* 2:203–4), an amusing occasional piece that is notable only for its influence on Burns. This epistle, again in tetrameters, contains a refrainlike couplet in lines 5–6 that is repeated in lines 31–32:

Dight your Een, and cease your grieving,	*wipe; eyes*
ALLAN's hale, and well, and living. . . .	

The closing lines of Burns's "Tam Samson's Elegy" were clearly suggested by this tricky couplet:

Tell ev'ry social, honest billie   *fellow*
        To cease his grievin,
For yet, unskaith'd by Death's   *unharmed;*
        gleg gullie,   *quick knife*
            Tam Samson's livin![12]

In 1729 Ramsay reverted to his favorite "Habbie" stanza for his lively "Epistle to Mr. John Gay, Author of the Shepherd's Week, on hearing her Grace Dutchess of Queensberry commend some of his Poems" (*STS,* 2:109–12). Ramsay had long admired the work of Gay, especially his pastorals, and had been influenced by him in important ways. In a letter to Sir John Clerk he called him enthusiastically "The Best of Poets" (*STS,* 4:185). John Gay made a visit to Scotland in the early summer of 1729 as the guest of the Duke of Queensberry, and it is almost certain that Ramsay met him in Edinburgh on that occasion. This epistle, a manuscript of which is dated 10 August 1729 (*STS,* 6:73–74), was very probably written shortly after Ramsay had made the English poet's acquaintance; certainly its familiar tone suggests such a sequence of events.

No doubt in deference to Gay, Ramsay's language in this verse letter is a kind of watered down Scots; he avoids the use of "braid" vernacular terms that would be difficult for his English friend. The third stanza illustrates the style:

Now, lend thy Lug, and tent me, GAY   *ear; heed*
Thy Fate appears like Flow'rs in May
Fresh flowrishing, and lasting ay,   *always*
        Firm as an Aik,   *oak*
Which envious Winds, when Criticks bray,
        Shall never shake.

Here the Scoto-English mode does not detract from the liveliness and wit that characterize the epistle as a whole. Ramsay goes on to explain that although Gay had already been much admired by Pope, Arbuthnot, and himself, he has now reached the pinnacle by being praised by the lovely "Clarinda" (Duchess of Queensberry). Inspired by this, Gay should soar to even greater poetic heights, and Ramsay in Edinburgh longs for the chance to visit him in London (stanza 15):

THUS sing,—whil'st I frae *Arthur*'s Height,	(*hill at Edinburgh*)
O'er *Chiviot* gowr with tyr'd Sight,	*Cheviot stare*
And langing wish, like raving Wight,	*longing*
To be set down,	
Frae Coach and sax, baith trim and tight,	*six, both*
In *London* Town.	

Altogether, the "Epistle to Gay" is a fine poem, in good taste and good humor; it is witty without straining for effects, and must be ranked among the most accomplished of Ramsay's Scots epistles.

In the mid 1730s Ramsay produced two more epistles that are worthy of comment. "Address of Thanks from the Society of Rakes" (*STS,* 3:128–34), published by Ramsay anonymously in 1735 in pamphlet form, is a facetious and mildly bawdy epistle to the Reverend "Philosark," a young Scottish minister, Daniel MacLauchlan of Ardnamurchan, who had published a tract ironically advocating fornication in the manner of Swift's *A Modest Proposal.* [13] For this rather lengthy piece (180 lines) Ramsay used the verse form of his "Epistle to Forbes." A single stanza, the third, will suffice to exemplify the style:

Now Lads laugh a', and take your Wills,	
And scowp around like Tups and Bulls,	*leap quickly; rams*
Have at the bony Lasses;	
For Conscience has nae mair to say,	*no more*
Our *Clergy-man* has clear'd the Way,	
And proven our Fathers Asses.	

Here, and elsewhere in spots, Ramsay's address is fairly witty and imaginative.

Passing over several other verse letters of trivial import, we may turn finally to Ramsay's "Epistle to John Wardlaw" (*STS,* 3:238–40), dating from June 1736. This is an entertaining piece in tetrameter couplets that Ramsay for some reason left unpublished; it was not printed until long after his death when it appeared in the *Scots Magazine* in 1797.[14] Here Ramsay writes to an old friend who managed a country estate, asking for the cash payment of overdue interest on a bond. The comic theme of this epistle is that whereas country folk can always find food

and clothing of their own growth, townspeople (like Ramsay)
must have ready cash or else they starve. He reminds Wardlaw
that city dwellers must have money for rent, food, drink, clothes,
and children's schooling (lines 21–24):

All these require the ready down	*ready money*
Frae us that live in Borrowstown,	*a royal Burgh*
That neither hae nor barn, nor byre,	*have; cowshed*
Washing, nor elding for our fire. . . .	*fuel*

Farming folk, on the other hand, can provide for themselves
(lines 29–34):

While ye jock upo' lands,	*rural fellows*
Have ilka thing laid to your hands	*every*
Of whatsoe'er ye stand in need,	
Of your ain growth and your ain breed.	*own*
Frae udders of your kine and ewes	*cows*
Your cream, your cheese, your butter flows. . . .	

Note that the Scots pronunciation of "ewes" as "yowes" makes
this last rhyme almost identical. The "Epistle to Wardlaw," altogether, is a charming piece of work in Ramsay's relaxed, earthy
style.

Horatian Odes in Scots

Burns Martin's assertion that "Ramsay spoke a great truth
when he said that he understood Horace but faintly in the
original"[15] is a wry understatement. Ramsay's Latin was indeed
shaky. In the manuscript "Life of Allan Ramsay," probably by
his son, we are told that "he much lamented his deficiency in
the Latin; of which, however, he had pickt up so much, as, by
the help of Dacier [a French translator of Horace], to catch
the spirit of the Odes of Horace; which, even by this twilight,
he, above all writings, admired; and, supplying, by congenial
fancy, what he wanted in erudition, had imitated some of them
with a truly Horatian felicity" (*STS,* 4:73). Kinghorn is probably
right in speculating that Ramsay's knowledge of Horace came
directly through one of the English translations of Dacier's

French version (*STS,* 4:110). At any rate, the depth of the
linguistic "twilight" in which Ramsay undertook to "translate"
Horace can be seen at its worst in the motto that he prefixed
to his poem on the South Sea Bubble, "Wealth, or the Woody"
(*STS,* 1:152). Ramsay gives first the lines from Horace, which
read, in part, "qui fragilem truci / Commisit pelago ratem /
Primus," for which a flat literal translation would be "who first
ventured a fragile boat upon the rough sea." Ramsay then presents his Scots rendering as follows:

> Wha ventur'd first upon the Sea
> With Hempen Branks, and Horse of Tree.   *halter; wood*

Where in Horace's straightforward clause did Ramsay find his
wooden horse and rope halter? Not only is this an absurd distortion of Horace's lines, but it is bad poetry in its own right.
This monstrosity, however, is not a fair sample of Ramsay's
free adaptations of Horace's odes, some of which are, as his
son stated, quite felicitous.

Ramsay plunged into the task of paraphrasing about half a
dozen of Horace's odes early in his career, about the same
time that he became involved in the Horatian verse epistle.
He was attracted to the Latin poet for the reasons given at
the beginning of this chapter, and also because he wished to
dignify his image as a Scots poet among the well-educated Edinburgh literati. That he was understandably unsure of himself
(a rare thing in Ramsay) is indicated by the fact that when he
published the first collected edition of *Poems* (1721) he tucked
away all of his versions of Horace's odes at the very end of
the volume. As it turned out, he need not have been so worried.

Probably all of Ramsay's significant Horatian odes were composed about 1719 or 1720, and most were included in his quarto
volume of 1721.[16] We have already noticed his vigorous rendering of Horace, *Odes,* book 1, ode 11, incorporated into his
third epistle to William Hamilton, which may well have been
his earliest attempt at the genre. "To the Right Honourable,
William Earl of Dalhousie" (*STS,* 1:217–19), in tetrameter couplets, is a *very* loose adaptation of Horace, *Odes,* book 1, ode
1, but is fairly interesting and competent. Considerably better
is "An Ode to Mr. F———" (*STS,* 1:221–22), also in tetrameters

and probably addressed to John Forbes of Newhall. This is a
free rendering of *Odes,* book 1, ode 4, and is marked by what
Kinghorn praises as Ramsay's "eager grasp of the concrete"
(*STS,* 4:111). Here, for example, is Ramsay's version, in part,
of Horace's comment on the levelling power of Death (lines
27–30);

That ill bred Death has nae Regard	*no*
To King or Cottar, or a Laird,	*cottager; landowner*
As soon a Castle he'll attack,	
As Waus of Divots roof'd wi' Thack.	*walls; turf; thatch*

The rich vernacular Scots in the details here and throughout
the ode works surprisingly well in approximating the terseness
and texture of Horace's style.

Another interesting attempt is "The Poet's Wish: An Ode"
(*STS,* 1:243–44), an adaptation of *Odes,* book 1, ode 31, in
which Ramsay experiments with the Middle Scots stanza form
of Alexander Montgomerie's *The Cherrie and the Slae.* This difficult fourteen-line stanza Ramsay manages with a moderate level
of skill; in this one he sticks closely to the content and spirit
of Horace's ode, while at the same time he gives it a distinctively
Scottish flavor, with references to the Tay and Tweed and the
Grampians, and with "hamely" imagery as in the opening lines
of the last stanza:

For me I can be well content	
To eat my Bannock on the Bent,	*oaten bread; field*
And kitchen't wi' fresh Air;	*flavor it*
Of Lang-kail I can make a Feast,	*cabbage*
And cantily had up my Crest,	*happily hold up*
And laugh at Dishes rare.	

In "To R—— H—— B——, an Ode" (*STS,* 1:231–32), probably addressed to Sir John Clerk who as Baron of Exchequer
was called "Right Honourable Baron" by the poet,[17] Ramsay
went back to the "Habbie" stanza for this paraphrase of *Odes,*
book 1, ode 18. Here we have a rather free adaptation of Horace's brief celebration of wine, with several vigorous expansions

of the original text. Stanza 6 is typical, on the foolishness of excessive drinking:

> Let's set these Hair-brain'd Fowk in View,   *folk*
> That when they're stupid, mad and fow   *drunk*
> Do brutal Deeds, which aft they rue
>   For a' their Days,
> Which frequently prove very few
>   To such as these.

Ramsay's strong, earthy images transform Horace's smooth, succinct ode into something quite different—more concrete, more lively, but less brilliant stylistically.

The longest, best-known, and most successful of Ramsay's Horatian odes is entitled "To the Ph—— —— an Ode" (*STS*, 1:223–25), based on *Odes*, book 1, ode 9. Very probably this one is addressed to the Phiz Club, an Edinburgh society to which several of Ramsay's distinguished friends belonged.[18] It is composed in tetrameter quatrains (*a b a b*) and is a very "free" rendering of the original. The opening lines, on the Pentland Hills on the southern outskirts of Edinburgh, enjoy a modest fame:

> Look up to *Pentland*'s towring Taps,   *tops*
> Buried beneath great Wreaths of Snaw,   *snow*
> O'er ilka Cleugh, ilk Scar and Slap,   *cleft; gully; gap*
> As high as ony *Roman* Wa'.   *wall*

In the midst of frigid winter, the zestful conviviality indoors in Auld Reekie (Edinburgh) is beautifully suggested in stanza 3:

> Then fling on Coals, and ripe the Ribs,   *clear the grate*
> And beek the House baith   *warm;*
>   Butt and Ben,   *outer and inner rooms*
> That Mutchken Stoup it hads   *pint mug; holds;*
>   but Dribs,   *drops*
> Then let's get in the tappit Hen.   *half-gallon tankard*

This is a brilliant stanza, irresistible in its exuberance, full of a graphic colloquial vitality. Ramsay's use of Scots vernacular terms for drinking measures here is especially effective. Kinghorn, in his judicious discussion of all of Ramsay's adaptations of Horace's odes, praises this as "one of the best examples of a successful attempt on Ramsay's part to re-create the naive Horatian Epicureanism" (*STS,* 4:110). The entire ode is as vigorous as the stanzas just cited and it is, at the same time, carefully crafted with no stylistic blunders. It may not quite be Horace, but it is Ramsay at his best, and that is very good.

The poems discussed above by no means exhaust the list of Ramsay's "translations" of Horace—several others could be mentioned[19]—but they suffice to illustrate the range of his adaptations (from close to very free renderings of the Latin texts), and they comprise the best of his work in this genre.

Summary

Ramsay's Scots epistles and odes, based sometimes vaguely, sometimes specifically, on the work of Horace, are historically significant in the evolution of Scots poetry. His prolific work in the Scots verse epistle, stimulated by William Hamilton of Gilbertfield, was especially important in establishing a new, distinctively Scottish genre that he passed on to Fergusson and Burns and that became a major poetic form for the whole of the eighteenth century and beyond. Quite apart from their historic value, the best of Ramsay's Scots epistles—"Answer III" to William Hamilton and the epistles to Forbes and Gay—are delightful and admirable poems in their own right.

The Horatian odes in Scots are interesting as part of Ramsay's campaign to elevate Scottish verse to a higher level of dignity and respect among the intelligentsia, and to make it once again a part of European literature. Artistically, Ramsay's Scots odes are less valuable on the whole than his epistles, though at least one of them—the ode beginning "Look up to *Pentland's* towring Taps"—is a very fine piece of work indeed.

Chapter Four

Scots Pastorals

In the first phase of his career Allan Ramsay began to experiment in the classical pastoral tradition, and his Scots poems about the lives and loves of shepherds and shepherdesses had surprising and crucial results for Scottish literature. In the native tradition, the Middle Scots poet Robert Henryson had produced in "Robene and Makyne" (ca. 1480) the earliest known pastoral poem in British literature, and Ramsay certainly knew this piece from his study in 1718 of the Bannatyne Manuscript. But his real opportunity came through the fashionable vogue of pastoralism in his own time, as filtered through English Augustan poets such as Alexander Pope and, especially, John Gay. Beginning with pastoral elegies, Ramsay produced the first serious verse in the Scots tongue for over a century, and in so doing he greatly enlarged the possibilities for the use of Scots as a poetic language in his own day and in the future. Beyond that, in the years from 1720 to 1723 Ramsay composed three pastoral love eclogues out of which grew his master work, *The Gentle Shepherd* (1724), a pastoral drama that became the essential foundation for modern Scottish pastoralism.

Pastoral Elegies in Scots

Quite early in his career, in 1719, Ramsay produced his first pastoral poem in Scots, "Richy and Sandy, A Pastoral on the Death of Joseph Addison, Esq." (*STS,* 1:106–11). No doubt he was encouraged in his use of language by the popular success of John Gay's pastoral *The Shepherd's Week* (1714), in which rustic idiom had been judiciously employed;[1] but Ramsay's choice of Scots for this elegy was, nevertheless, a daring one. Gay's work, with its sprinkling of English dialectal vocabulary, was, after all, intended to amuse his readers with its comic realism and ironic tone. But Ramsay's poem is wholly serious in subject matter and intent; Scots had not been used for such poetic purposes since the sixteenth century, as we have seen, and Ramsay here was breaking new ground. That he was well aware of the risk he was taking is shown by the fact that he had his English friend Josiah Burchett compose "An Explanation of Richy and Sandy." This is, in fact, a verse paraphrase in standard English which Ramsay published in small print as footnotes to his poem in case his "braid Scots" diction might be unintelligible to some readers.

Historically, then, "Richy and Sandy" is a bold and important innovation; but artistically it is a dubious performance. The basic problem is that Ramsay's characterization is unconvincing. In this poem Joseph Addison is called *"Edie,"* Sir Richard Steele is "Richy," and Alexander Pope is "Sandy"—and all three are represented as Scottish shepherds. The gap between the reader's concepts of these great urban (and urbane) writers and Ramsay's rustics and his "hamely" Scots style is too great, so that the poem strikes one as lacking in good taste and as slightly absurd. The classical allusions that Ramsay introduces ("Had [hold] up my Heart O Pan!") are sometimes poorly integrated.

Even with these serious flaws, however, "Richy and Sandy" is not a total failure. The elegy has some passages of genuine freshness and charm. Near the beginning Richy guesses at the possible causes of Sandy's woes: a falling out with his lass, a fright from a "Bogle," or a favorite wether (castrated ram) breaking a leg. Sandy replies (lines 11–14) that the case is far more serious:

> Naithing like that, sic troubles eith were   *such; easily*
>   born,
> What's Bogles,—Wedders,—or what's
>   *Mausy's* Scorn?
> Our loss is meikle mair, and past Remeed,   *much more; remedy*
> *Edie,* that play'd and sang sae sweet, is
>   dead.

There is a disarming simplicity and naturalness about such lines that help to redeem a poem that suffers from a distortion of realities—a basic unnaturalness.

This pioneer pastoral elegy in Scots was soon followed by

another in the same verse form (pentameter couplets) and format, "Keitha: A Pastoral, Lamenting the Death of the Right Honourable Mary Countess of Wigtoun" (*STS*, 1:204–7), apparently composed in 1721.[2] Again Ramsay has two shepherds as his speakers, "Ringan" and "Colin." The following lines (81–84), spoken by Ringan, will illustrate the style of this lament for an aristocratic lady:

The Lasses wha did at her Graces mint,	*aim*
Ha'e by her Death their bonniest pattern tint.	*lost*
O ilka ane, who did her Bounty skair,	*everyone; share*
Lament, for gen'rous Keitha is nae mair.	*no more*

The elegy is more natural than "Richy and Sandy" in one sense—that is, it is not impaired by the dignified connotations of names like Addison, Steele, and Pope. On the other hand, Ramsay's style in "Keitha" is generally somewhat stiff, with a feeling of strain that is absent from his first Scots elegy—as we can see in the lines cited above. Worse, there is a passage on Keitha's relations with her husband (lines 55–66) that is in very poor taste; the elegy as a whole must be judged as mediocre.

Much more successful is "Robert, Richy, and Sandy; A Pastoral on the Death of Matthew Prior, Esq." (*STS*, 2:18–22), composed in 1721. In this pastoral elegy "Robert" is Robert Harley, Earl of Oxford, and, as in "Richy and Sandy," the idea of Oxford, Steele, and Pope in shepherd disguise, speaking in Scots, is faintly ludicrous to modern readers. In other respects, however, this is an attractive poem and shows improvement in Ramsay's pastoral technique. An interesting difference from the two earlier elegies is that in this one Ramsay approximates the traditional "eclogue" form. The eclogue normally is a poem consisting of dialogue between two or more characters, enclosed within a narrative framework. The elegies on Addison and Mary Keith had been simply dialogues without the framework; that on Prior has a narrative prologue (lines 1–18). Furthermore, Ramsay here employs a refrain device in the central section of the poem (lines 43–104) which, though slightly artificial, is rather pleasing. Five of the speeches of Richy and Sandy end with a varying

refrain line—"How blyth he was? how much lamented fell?"
"How wise he was? how much lamented fell?" and so forth.
The style of this elegy is a delicate fusion of the artificial
and the "hamely," so that a certain level of dignity is carefully
maintained. The last part of Richy's second speech (lines 55–
60), where he recounts the blowing down of a stately ash tree,
is typical:

> But ae rough Night the blat'ring Winds
>   blew snell,   *sharp*
> Torn frae its Roots, adown it souchan fell;   *sighing*
> Twin'd of its Nourishment, it lifeless lay,   *separated from*
> Mixing its wither'd Leaves amang the Clay.
> Sae flowrish'd *Matt:* But where's the Tongue
>   can tell
> How fair he grew? How much lamented fell?

Here, and throughout the elegy, we have a very skillful stylistic
compromise, with just enough vernacular diction to give a sad-
sweet Scottish flavor to what is, altogether, a fine and sensitive
tribute to Matthew Prior.

Ramsay's last pastoral elegy in Scots was composed in 1732
and entitled "Kate and Susan, A Pastoral to the Memory of
John Gay, Esqr." (*STS,* 3:225–29). For some reason the poet
chose never to publish this substantial tribute (135 lines), yet
it is a solid and creditable performance. As in "Robert, Richy,
and Sandy," Ramsay here uses the classical eclogue form with
a brief narrative introduction (lines 1–9) in rather pedestrian
tetrameters; the main body of the poem, the dialogue between
"Katty" and Susan, is in the "Habbie" stanza. The conversation
opens in stereotyped fashion with Katty noting that Susan is
"begrutten" (in tears) and asking the reason for her grief. Susan
explains as follows (lines 28–33):

> He's dead! Oh Kattie, Johny's dead,
> Wha daintily coud tune his reed
> To please the brugh and chear the mead.   *town; country*
>   Nane drave away
> The dronan frumps wi' faster speed   *groaning*
>   Than Johny Gay.

After this fairly spirited beginning Ramsay goes on to pay his respects to Gay in specific terms. He praises the English poet for his efforts (in *The Beggar's Opera* and elsewhere) to rejuvenate native music—"Blyth British tunes"—in opposition to the fashionable craze for Italian melodies, a struggle in which Ramsay himself, as we shall see, was a valiant participant. More boldly, Ramsay recalls Gay's courage in subjecting all classes of society, from "porter" to "peer," to the attacks of his satiric pen, and for his resistance to the blandishments of lordly patrons offering servile sinecures (lines 64–81). He laments the passing of the author of *The Shepherd's Week,* and of *The Beggar's Opera* in which Gay dared to expose the corruptions of the ruling class—"Thieves that under Coro'nets hide" (line 106). Finally, Ramsay puts in the mouth of "Katty" his praise of Gay's *Trivia,* a poem on the art of walking the streets of London, and of his *Fables,* derived from Aesop (lines 112–23):

His Roundels a' were snod and sweet,	*neat*
Well taught he how to wawk the Street,	*walk*
On drouthy Days, in Wind and Weet,	*dry*
His Sonnet Tells;	
How we frae mischiefs we might meet,	
Should shield our Sells.	*ourselves*
Like snacky Easop too right slee,	*clever; sly*
He with a' Ranks of Men made free,	
And wyl'd us frae our fau'ts wi' Glee	*took us away; faults*
And Moral Saws;	
Mair pithy, Men of Sense agree,	*powerful*
Than stonkard Laws.	*sullen*

Why did Ramsay choose not to print this memorable elegy? A relevant fact is that the poem shows signs of careful revision after a slapdash preliminary version that survives in the Egerton Manuscript (see *STS,* 6:145–8). In poems that Ramsay clearly intended for private circulation only, he was habitually careless, not bothering much with conventional spelling, punctuation, or capitalization. In this one, however, he obviously took pains to produce a fair copy, as though he originally meant it for publication. Probably Ramsay changed his mind in this instance because he feared that the elegy, with its outspoken praise of

Gay's satires on the aristocracy, might give offense to some of
his high-born friends. At any rate, "Kate and Susan" is a good
poem. It has a kind of subdued wit that makes it less entirely
serious in mood than "Robert, Richy, and Sandy," but it deserves to be ranked with that elegy as among Ramsay's better
serious poems in Scots.

Pastoral Love Eclogues in Scots

Between 1720 and 1723 Ramsay composed three Scots pastoral love eclogues: "Patie and Roger" (March 1720), "Patie
and Pegie" (1720), and "Jenny and Meggy" (1723). Since all
three eventually became integral parts of *The Gentle Shepherd,*
which will be discussed in detail later in this chapter, they need
not delay us long here. Nevertheless, the three eclogues were
originally written as separate, individual poems, before Ramsay
had even conceived of *The Gentle Shepherd,* and as such they
have significance as steps in the evolution of his pastoral technique and as background to his master work.

Encouraged, no doubt, by the favorable reception of his first
pastoral elegy of "Richy and Sandy" (1719), Ramsay attempted
in the next year a more ambitious experiment with "Patie and
Roger: A Pastoral Inscrib'd to Josiah Burchet, Esq; Secretary
of the Admiralty" (*STS,* 1:138–48). Two editions of this piece
were published in 1720 in pamphlet form, one in Edinburgh
and one in London, prior to its inclusion in *Poems* (1721). The
existence of the London edition shows that, even as early as
this, Ramsay, with the help of Burchett and other English admir-
ers, was aspiring to an all-British audience and reputation. With
his characteristic shrewdness, he perceived a unique opportunity
for a Scottish poet in the current vogue of pastoralism in the
English capital. John Gay's use of colloquial English dialect in
The Shepherd's Week had been not only acceptable but widely
popular in London; perhaps, then, pastoral poems in Scots would
be even more distinctive and at least equally charming to this
wider reading public. Ramsay saw his chance and exploited it
brilliantly.

"Patie and Roger," with 54 lines of dedication and 168 lines
of eclogue, is Ramsay's lengthiest work in the pastoral mode

prior to *The Gentle Shepherd.* The dedication to Josiah Burchett is in the "Habbie" stanza; it is a competent but poetically bland piece of routine flattery, though the final stanza is deftly handled:

May never Care your Blessings sowr,	*sour*
And may the Muses ilka Hour	*every*
Improve your Mind, and Haunt your Bower:	
I'm but a Callan:	*young fellow*
Yet may I please you, while I'm your	
Devoted ALLAN.	

This is not bad, but the eclogue that follows is much livelier.

Ramsay opens his eclogue with a brief, seven-line narrative prologue. He has used this kind of structure earlier in "A Tale of Three Bonnets," but this is his first attempt at it in the pastoral convention. The prologue sets the scene and introduces the two characters succinctly, with effective "hamely" detail—a technique Ramsay was to adopt later in setting his scenes throughout *The Gentle Shepherd.* The ensuing dialogue between Patie and Roger is richly colloquial and vigorous. Its structure is especially interesting. Whereas in traditional pastoral (as in "Richy and Sandy") the reason for a character's grief is revealed in his first speech, in this conversation Ramsay keeps us waiting and builds a degree of suspense. Only gradually and through repeated questioning by Patie does Roger admit that the cause of his despair is Jenny's rejection of his love. At the same time in the course of this step by step confession, Ramsay works into the dialogue many realistic details of shepherd life and revealing suggestions of the contrasting personalities of Patie and Roger. In short, the eclogue is an effective piece of dramatic writing; Ramsay builds an interesting scene with unobstrusive skill, and he manages to create an illusion of naturalness and truth to life that is quite convincing.

From a stylistic point of view "Patie and Roger" is equally successful, with several memorable phrases that were to find echoes in the work of both Fergusson and Burns.[3] In this poem Ramsay is more daring than in "Rich and Sandy" in his use of "plain braid Scots," a fact that is the more remarkable when we recall that he was consciously aiming to appeal to London as well as to Edinburgh. In any case, the results are felicitous, especially in Patie's long, very quotable speech (lines 103–40) of which the opening couplets read as follows:

Daft Gowk! Leave aff that silly	*silly fool;*
whindging Way,	*whining*
Seem careless, there's my Hand ye'll win	
the Day.	
Last Morning I was unco airly out,	*very early*
Upon a Dyke I lean'd and glowr'd about;	*stone wall; stared*
I saw my Meg come linkan o'er the Lee,	*walking*
I saw my Meg, but Maggie saw na me;	
For yet the Sun was wading throw the Mist,	*through*
And she was closs upon me e'er she wist.	*close; knew*

The rest of the speech, and indeed most of the eclogue, is as good as this, with a vernacular vitality and undeniable charm. This is Ramsay's Scots verse at its best.

The success of "Patie and Roger" was followed up almost immediately by "Patie and Pegie: A Sang" (*STS*, 1:183–84). It is a much briefer effort, more or less in the form of a pastoral love eclogue but without the narrative framework; it is a kind of two-part song, with Patie and Pegie taking turns at a stanza each through five stanzas and then joining together in a chorus at the end. "Patie and Pegie" later became incorporated in the original version of *The Gentle Shepherd* as the last part of act 2, scene 4, and served as the singing finale for the second act. Ramsay's language in this dialogue is Scoto-English instead of the rich, colloquial Scots of "Patie and Roger," and, partly because of that, the song is poetically weaker, though not without touches of genteel but pleasing wit, especially in the final chorus.

Vastly more important is Ramsay's third attempt at the pastoral love eclogue in Scots, published separately as a pamphlet in 1723, entitled "Jenny and Meggy. A Pastoral, Being a Sequel to Patie and Roger."[4] It consists of eight lines of narrative prologue, followed by 207 lines of dialogue, all of which were destined to form act 1, scene 2 of *The Gentle Shepherd*. In all of these poems, incidentally, and in the pastoral play itself, the heroine is the same person, though called by various names— "Pegie," "Meg," "Meggy," "Maggy," all of which are nick-

names for Margaret; in *The Gentle Shepherd* "Peggy" predomi-
nates. The structure of "Jenny and Meggy" is roughly parallel
to that of "Patie and Roger," except that in the former we
have a debate on the subject of marriage, with Jenny sneering
at its risks and potential miseries and Meggy stressing its joys.
The opposed attitudes of the two lasses are neatly contrasted
in their views on having children. Jenny, in lines 110–13, scorns
the prospect with bitter sarcasm:

O! 'tis a pleasant thing to be a Bride;	
Syne whindging Getts about your Ingle-side,	*then whining children; fire-*
Yelping for this or that with fasheous Din,	*troublesome*
To mak them Brats then ye maun toil and spin.	*rags; must*

Meggy views the same situation in a light that is exactly the
contrary of Jenny's (lines 118–21):

Yes, 'tis a heartsome thing to be a Wife,	
When round the Ingle-edge young Sprouts are rife.	*fire-*
Gif I'm sae happy, I shall have delight,	*if*
To hear their little Plaints, and keep them right.	

The contrast between the two women in this passage and
throughout the dialogue is fairly effective dramatically, but Ramsay has Jenny persist in her opinion to an extent that seems
somewhat unnatural. The Scots idiom in this eclogue, too, is
slightly watered down as compared to "Patie and Roger,"
though there are some fresh and delightful lines.

Altogether, "Jenny and Meggy" with "Patie and Roger" represent a new kind of achievement in Scottish pastoralism. Ramsay
succeeds in these substantial eclogues in blending the artificial
conventions of classical pastoral with an unexpected realism and
a modest dramatic skill. His settings and characters are slightly
idealized, of course, but they give the impression of being not
far removed from real country folk. The language itself helps
immensely in creating this effect of relative naturalness. In these
poems Ramsay shrewdly hit upon a linguistic compromise and

a careful balance of realism and romance that were just right, and that gave him the confidence to move ahead to achieve the astonishing success, among all classes of readers, of *The Gentle Shepherd.*

The Gentle Shepherd

This pastoral drama, Ramsay's longest and most important original creation, has had an unusually checkered career in literary history and criticism. Though it enjoyed a huge popularity in Ramsay's lifetime and throughout the eighteenth century, it fared but poorly in the hands of the genteel literati of the Scottish Enlightenment—such snobbish critics as James Beattie (1776), Hugh Blair (1783), and, most notoriously, John Pinkerton (1786)—all of whom deplored what they stigmatized as its "vulgarity."[5] At the end of the century, however, this prevailing critical tendency was suddenly reversed by the glowingly favorable essay of Lord Woodhouselee in 1800.[6] What happened between 1786 and 1800 to account for this sudden shift in the scholarly assessment of *The Gentle Shepherd?* Apart from differences in the minds and personalities of the critics involved, surely a crucial factor was the rise of Burns to international fame in these years, a development that suddenly made Scottish poetry respectable once again in the loftiest critical circles. Following Woodhouselee the critical tone shifted to one of extravagant overpraise that persisted through most of the nineteenth century. William Tennant, writing in 1852, went so far as to call *The Gentle Shepherd* "one of the best pastoral dramas in the wide circle of European literature."[7] In the twentieth century critical opinion generally has shifted once again toward a downgrading of the play. Most commentators have followed the lead of Thomas F. Henderson who, in 1898, reasserted the old charge of "vulgarity" and lack of sophistication.[8] This view has generally prevailed in recent times, with, at best, rather grudging and qualified praise in the work of such critics as David Daiches, Maurice Lindsay, and Alexander Kinghorn.[9] In the most recent study of all, however, that of Thomas Crawford, a thorough and judicious analysis, we see once again a movement in the opposite direction toward a more balanced and historically fair evaluation of this remarkable play.[10]

Allan Ramsay composed *The Gentle Shepherd* during the years 1724 and 1725, finishing it on 29 April of the latter year as he tells us himself in a whimsical note in the original manuscript: "finished the 29th of Aprile 1725 just as eleven aclock strikes by All. Ramsay All Glory be to God Amen" (*STS*, 6:97). The idea for the play grew, as we have seen, from the germ of Ramsay's two eclogues, "Patie and Roger" and "Jenny and Meggy," and it was first published in 1725 by the author. In its original version *The Gentle Shepherd* contained only four songs, including the earlier "Patie and Pegie"; three years later, encouraged by the phenomenal success of Gay's *The Beggar's Opera* (1728), Ramsay added many new songs (to a total of twenty), and in so doing transformed his pastoral play into a ballad-opera, a change that he later regretted (*STS*, 4:72–73). In the present discussion the play will be treated as it appeared in its original form; the songs added later are taken up in the next chapter.

The full title of Ramsay's drama is *The Gentle Shepherd, A Pastoral Comedy; Inscrib'd to the Right Honourable, Susanna Countess of Eglintoun.* It begins with a dedication to this patroness in fulsome, flattering prose (*STS*, 2:205–6); this is followed in the second edition of 1726 and in subsequent editions by a second dedication, written by Ramsay's friend and fellow poet William Hamilton of Bangour, in fairly competent English heroic couplets, recommending the work to the Countess of Eglintoun (*STS*, 2:207–11). Then comes a list of "The Persons" and, finally, the text of the play (*STS* 2:213–77). Except for the songs, some of the prologues, and one or two special passages, the whole of the play is composed in pentameter couplets; and, apart from some of the speeches of the aristocrat Sir William Worthy, all of it is in Scots.

The general literary background to Ramsay's Scots pastoralism has already been touched upon, but some comment relating specifically to *The Gentle Shepherd* seems desirable here. In his chapter on this play Thomas Crawford has given us an expert summary of the entire history of European pastoral poetry, tracing its evolution from the ancient Greek poet Theocritus (third century B.C.), through the Roman Virgil to the Renaissance Italian and English poets (especially Spenser), and finally to Ramsay's English contemporaries.[11] Ramsay's Scots pastorals as a whole are obviously related to the great debate in France and England in the late seventeenth and early eighteenth centuries as to the extent to which the classical Greek and Roman genre of the pastoral should be "domesticated"—that is, given local settings and characters instead of the traditional Italian or Arcadian ones, and given some degree of native colloquialism in the style. In this argument Ramsay was clearly on the side of domestication, wherein he saw a special opportunity for the use of Scots. His English precedents in the use of dialectal speech were, obviously, Gay's *Shepherd's Week* and the poems of Ambrose Philips,[12] to which Crawford would add the English pastorals of Thomas Purney (published in 1716–17) which included a fair amount of dialectal vocabulary.[13]

All recent critics of *The Gentle Shepherd* have pointed out Ramsay's debt to English pastoral poetry, but a wholly different kind of influence has been totally ignored—that of English sentimental comedy, then at the height of its popularity in London. One of Ramsay's favorite authors, Sir Richard Steele, had just published in 1722 his last and best play, *The Conscious Lovers,* the quintessential comedy of serious sentiment; and it seems extremely probable that Ramsay would have known this play (and others like it) and have been affected by it in the composition of *The Gentle Shepherd.* Commentators on Ramsay's drama, by concentrating exclusively on the pastoral background, have missed this entire other area of influence. A close look at the text will show, among other things, the important impact of sentimental comedy.

The two scenes that form act 1 of *The Gentle Shepherd* are simply reprintings of Ramsay's earlier love eclogues, "Patie and Roger" and "Jenny and Meggy," of which we have already seen a few characteristic passages. The first scene opens with a neat prologue, the most effective of the fifteen in the play:

Beneath the South side of a Craigy Beild,	*rocky shelter*
Where Crystal Springs the halesome Waters yield,	*wholesome*
Twa youthful Shepherds on the Gowans lay,	*daisies*
Tenting their Flocks ae bonny Morn of May.	*watching*
Poor *Roger* granes till hollow Echoes ring:	*groans*
But blyther *Patie* likes to laugh and sing.	

Here Ramsay deftly establishes the linguistic blend of braid Scots and English "poetic" idiom that prevails throughout the work and ensured its popularity among both gentry and common folk.

In the first scene the characters of Patie and Roger are skillfully contrasted. Patie is a poor shepherd, but handsome, accomplished, cheerful, and sensible; he is in love with Peggy, who returns his passion. Roger, on the other hand, is a relatively rich shepherd with a large flock; he too is handsome, but very shy and in despair over Jenny's disdain. Patie wisely advises him that Jenny's coyness is affected rather than real, and that Roger's best strategy would be to pretend indifference himself (lines 141–24):

> Seem to forsake her, soon she'll change her Mood;
> Gae woo anither, and she'll gang clean wood.   *go mad*

We also learn that Jenny supposedly loves Bauldy, but Bauldy "sighs for *Neps.*"[14] The whole scene is a pleasing example of old-fashioned (or rather, universal) diplomacy in courtship.

In the second scene Peggy asks Jenny why she rejects Roger, and Jenny replies (lines 35–36):

> I dinna like him, *Peggy,* there's an end;
> A *Herd* mair sheepish yet I never kend.   *shepherd*

The rest of the scene then turns into a spirited debate on marriage, with Peggy urging Jenny not to waste her chances. Jenny asserts (line 55), "I never thought a single Life a Crime," to which Peggy answers:

> Nor I—but Love in Whispers lets us ken,   *know*
> That Men were made for us, and we for Men.

Throughout this dialogue Peggy's attitude is hopeful and trusting, Jenny's is bitter and suspicious until, at the end, she admits that Peggy is probably right. Together these two scenes comprising act 1 are simple but dramatically effective. They function well to establish the circumstances and personalities of Ramsay's two sets of lovers; and they have a genuine freshness and charm in themselves.

In act 2 Ramsay moves his slender plot forward with despatch. The locale is the Pentland Hills near Edinburgh; the date is 1660, the year of the restoration of King Charles II after the Cromwell usurpation. In the opening scene we are introduced to Glaud and Symon, two old Midlothian farmers who meet outside Glaud's cottage. Symon (the supposed father of Patie) tells his good friend Glaud (father of Jenny and supposed "uncle" to Peggy) the good news that the king is restored and that their old laird, Sir William Worthy, long exiled in France with the king, is returning to his estate. The two old shepherds are jubilant: they have suffered under a cruel temporary landlord, and are happy that Sir William will once again enjoy his own property. Glaud adds (lines 42–45):

And may he lang; for never did he stent	*hinder*
Us in our thriving, with a racket Rent:	*excessive*
Nor grumbl'd, if ane grew rich;	
or shor'd to raise	*threatened*
Our Mailens, when we pat on *Sunday*'s Claiths.	*rents*

In this praise of an ideal laird Ramsay indirectly gives us a glimpse of the harsh realities in the lives of tenant farmers under less benevolent landowners. The scene ends with Glaud announcing that he will give a party, but Symon has already prepared one to celebrate the imminent return of their beloved Sir William.

In the next two scenes Ramsay introduces his subplot centered on Bauldy, a doltish fool. In soliloquy Bauldy reveals that he has fallen in love with Peggy and plans to ask the local witch, Mause, to cast a spell to enable him to break off with his current lass Neps, and to make Peggy love him. Scene 3, outside Mause's cottage, opens with the old woman singing to the traditional Scots tune of "Carle and the king come" a lyric that ranks among the best of Ramsay's Scots songs (lines 5–12):

> *Peggy*, now the King's come,
>   Peggy, now the King's come;
> Thou may dance, and I shall sing,
>   *Peggy*, since the King's come.

Nae mair the Hawkies shalt thou milk,   *cows*
But change thy Plaiding-Coat for silk,
And be a Lady of that Ilk,   *same place*
    Now, Peggy, since the King's come.

This excellent song serves a dramatic function in hinting at Peggy's gentle birth and in suggesting Mause's secret knowledge of it. At this point Bauldy enters and asks Mause to work her magic to straighten out his love life. Mause pretends to agree, but after Bauldy leaves she states in soliloquy that she resents his presumption and has other tales to tell.

Scene 4 of the second act is a chaste love talk between Patie and Peggy, in which each looks forward to their marriage. In the meantime, there will be no sex. This kind of discreet moral scene is wholly typical of sentimental comedy, in which the hero is amorous but restrained, the heroine willing but insistent upon the proprieties. Ramsay could have found the exact pattern for this in the scenes between Bevil Junior and Indiana in Steele's *The Conscious Lovers.*[15] At any rate, Ramsay's handling of the situation here has delicate grace, despite the basic artificiality. He ends the scene and the act with his previously written two-part song, "Patie and Pegie," an effective singing finale.

Ramsay begins act 3 with a prologue in neoclassical English with the slightest coloring of Scots—"Now turn your Eyes beyond yon spreading Lime, / And tent [pay attention to] a Man whase Beard seems bleech'd with Time"—and he does this in order to provide a stylistic transition to scene 1, a soliloquy in genteel English heroic couplets by Sir William Worthy. This shift in language strikes one as especially unnatural in a soliloquy (Sir William is thinking aloud). In real life a well educated Scottish laird of Ramsay's time, or in 1660, would probably have been capable of speaking in standard English on formal occasions, but he would certainly have been *thinking* in Scots. Ramsay is simply complying here with his culture's notions of class distinctions. Artistically, the results are unhappy: Sir William's speech is labored in style, no more than competent at best, as he reminisces about the former glories of his estate in hackneyed sentimental terms.

Scene 2, after another Scoto-English prologue, is much superior. Glaud, Symon, and Elspa (Symon's wife) are preparing to celebrate when Jenny enters with news of the arrival of a poor "spae-man" (fortune-teller) who is promptly welcomed to the party and is brought in by Patie. The old spae-man (Sir William in disguise) falls into a trance and predicts Patie's good fortune in inheriting a fine estate. In these speeches Sir William, playing the role of a beggar, expresses himself in braid Scots—and this time Ramsay comes closer to reality in the sense that the Scottish gentry of his century were, in fact, bilingual. It should be noted, though, that whereas Sir William speaks in his native tongue throughout the comical fortune-telling part of this scene, in his last speech (lines 158–61) when he turns to the serious business of arranging for a private talk with Symon he shifts into standard English.

In his next scene, after an awkward prologue, Ramsay presents a lively and dramatically sound dialogue between Roger and Jenny—a proposal scene that comes straight from the popular pattern of sentimental comedy. In this exchange Ramsay constructs neatly balanced and contrasting arguments, as in lines 38–41 where Jenny foresees the drudgery of housekeeping:

> When Prison'd in four Waws, a Wife right tame,   *walls*
> Altho' the first, the greatest Drudge at hame.   *home*

To which Roger responds:

> That only happens, when for sake of Gear,   *property*
> Ane wales a Wife, as he wad buy a Mear.   *chooses; mare*

Such a balanced conversational structure is contrived, of course, but it is nevertheless pleasing. The scene ends with Jenny agreeing to marry Roger, provided he is able to get her father Glaud's consent.

The third act closes with a scene between Sir William and Symon in which the laird reveals his true identity and questions Symon about Patie (whom he has left in Symon's care during his long exile). In this dialogue Symon speaks in Scots, Sir William in English colored only by an occasional native word or spelling. Symon gives a laudatory account of Patie's life and habits, especially his booklearning—Patie, he says, buys books whenever he goes to the Westport of Edinburgh to sell sheep.

Sir William is pleased with this news and pompously asserts that "Reading such Books can raise a Peasant's Mind / Above a Lord's that is not thus inclin'd." Ramsay's emphasis here and later in the play upon the value of reading and of self-education is a significant theme in *The Gentle Shepherd*. It reflects, of course, the poet's own experience—he had lifted himself from obscurity to fame and prosperity partly by virtue of such reading—and his genuine faith in the possibilities open to hard work and self-improvement. The democratic ideal of the "self-made" man has long been a powerful cultural force in Scotland, and Ramsay clearly believed in it. Sir William's liberal ideas on peasant education, however, do not extend into his notions of a fitting marriage for his son. He concludes that Patie must give up his "unambitious Fire" for the humble Peggy, and go on a grand tour of Europe to complete his education.

Act 4 opens with a scene of lively farce. Glaud's sister, Madge, tells Mause the news of the laird's return and his acknowledgment of Patie as his son. She feels sorry for Peggy in these circumstances (line 33): "Our *Meg,* poor thing, alake! has lost her Jo [sweetheart]." Mause, who has secret knowledge of Peggy's origins, is not so sure. At this point Bauldy enters, much encouraged in his pursuit of Peggy by the turn in events, and singing a snatch of the splendid folk song of rustic courtship, "Jocky said to Jenny." Madge accuses the clownish Bauldy of infidelity to Neps, Bauldy calls Madge a lying old maid, and a "stout Battle" breaks out in which Madge gives Bauldy a bloody nose. Bauldy takes to his heels, leaving Mause and Madge plotting to frighten him out of his wits by meeting him at night in disguise as witch and ghost. It is an effective scene of slapstick comedy.

The next scene is highly significant. Roger tells Patie of his success with Jenny; and Patie, now speaking in English with the faintest touch of Scots, recounts his meeting with his father in sentimental terms very reminiscent of similar passages in *The Conscious Lovers*.[16] Patie, in fact, is caught in the identical dilemma of Bevil Junior in Steele's play, torn between love and filial duty (Sir William has ordered him to forget about Peggy and to leave on an extended trip to London and then to France). And Patie faces the problem in exactly the same way as Bevil, by temporizing: he will accede to his father's wishes about the

trip, but will remain forever true to Peggy in his heart, and
will never marry a pampered aristocrat. In this brave speech
Patie reverts to his normal Scots (lines 58–63):

> Then 'tis design'd, when I can well behave,
> That I maun be some petted Thing's dull slave,   *must*
> For some few Bags of Cash, that I wat weel   *know*
> I need nae mair nor Carts do a third Wheel.   *more*
> But *Peggy*, dearer to me than my breath,
> Sooner than hear sic News, shall hear my Death.   *such*

Another highly interesting feature of this scene is in Patie's
satirical views of the life-style of the aristocracy. His comments
on their slothful luxury, pettiness, vicious backbiting, and general uselessness in lines 80–85 and 176–85 (see also those of
Glaud later in act 5, scene 2, lines 25–50), in contrast to the
healthful, productive life of the peasant—all of this looks forward
to Burns's fuller development of the theme in "The Twa Dogs"
and no doubt partly suggested it.[17] After Roger leaves, Peggy
arrives and Patie reassures her of his plans and faithful love.
This last part of the scene is, of course, very sentimental, with
both parties speaking in a watered-down Scoto-English, but it
is fairly well managed on the whole.
    Ramsay opens his final act with another farcical Bauldy scene.
Bauldy arrives before dawn at Symon's house in a state of panic
to tell Symon and Sir William that he has been beaten by the
witch, Mause, and by a "Ghaist" (Madge) raised by her. Sir
William scoffs at such silly superstitions among the country folk,
and this, too, was a comic theme that Ramsay passed on to
Burns who exploited it brilliantly in "Tam o' Shanter" (including some echoes of Ramsay's phrasing), "Address to the Deil,"
"Death and Dr. Hornbook," and other poems.[18] In his discussion of this scene Kinghorn deplores the fact that the audience
is denied the "promised comic scene" of Bauldy actually meeting the ghost, and must be satisfied with his report of the adventure. Kinghorn concludes from this that "Ramsay does not really
know how to write for the stage, and lacks the true dramatist's
consciousness of the power of witnessed as distinct from reported
action" (*STS*, 4:102–3). It is true, of course, that at the time
of composition of this play Ramsay had had little, if any, direct

experience with the theater; but he must have read a good number of plays, and he must have had *some* notion of the art. It is more likely that he considered putting the "Ghaist" scene on stage but decided against the idea, not because he was wholly ignorant about theatrical effects, but because doing so would interfere with his larger purposes. Very possibly he felt that the inclusion of a second scene of slapstick action, with Bauldy beaten up by women for a second time, would not only be too much of a good thing in itself, but would tend to dilute the serious mood of his play as a whole. *The Gentle Shepherd,* after all, is a serious sentimental comedy in the pastoral tradition; Ramsay did not want it to degenerate into farce. One of his main objectives, certainly, was to present a somewhat idealized and dignified picture of simple rural folk; too much of the hilarious boorishness of Bauldy would have destroyed that impression. We should note, in this connection, that Bauldy (and to a lesser extent Madge) is really the only "funny" character in the entire work. It would seem probable, then, that Ramsay made a conscious choice in this scene. Given that decision, his handling of it has vitality and shows considerable skill.

Scene 2 of the final act is brief but effective. Glaud fears that Patie, now that he is wealthy, will become a spoiled city rake, and he goes on to explain to the innocent Peggy and Jenny what that means. Madge arrives with the news that the quarrel between Bauldy and Mause is to be judged by Sir William at Symon's house. The scene ends with a lively dialogue between Madge and Peggy in which Madge jeers at Peggy over her misfortune, but Peggy holds her own with dignified patience (lines 69–70):

Dear Aunt, what need ye fash us wi' your Scorn?   *trouble*
That's no my Faut that I'm nae gentler born.   *fault*

In the last scene of *The Gentle Shepherd* all is revealed and all is resolved. Sir William judges Bauldy guilty of infidelity, and Bauldy promises to be true to Neps in future. The others arrive, and the laird notices in Peggy a strange resemblance to his dead sister. Glaud then explains that she was a foundling, left on his doorstep; and then Mause reveals her secret, that Peggy is the child of Sir William's sister, saved by her (Mause) from murderous relatives when she was a baby, and deposited at Glaud's. Now that Peggy is proven to be a gentlewoman by birth, Sir William agrees to her marriage with Patie; and then, at Patie's request, he gives his blessing to Roger and Jenny. All ends happily with Peggy's singing to the folk tune of "Cornriggs are bonny" a rousing song of virtuous love—"My *Patie* is a lover gay."

The ending of the play, with its extremely sentimental "recognition scene," is far from original. It is, in fact, very similar, once again, to the conclusion of Steele's *The Conscious Lovers,*[19] though it also bears a general resemblance to recognition scenes in countless comedies from earlier centuries—there must be over a dozen such scenes in Shakespeare alone. The obvious triteness of Ramsay's conclusion, however, has been overstressed in modern criticism and has tended to obscure the real nature and importance of his achievement.

The Gentle Shepherd was the first lengthy poetic work to be written in the Scots language since the sixteenth century, and as such it was epoch-making. No one today would argue that it is a great play; as Kinghorn rightly says, it has no immortal comic characters like Macheath or Polly Peachum in Gay's *Beggar's Opera;* but it is, nevertheless, surprisingly fresh and interesting in its genre. Kinghorn (*STS,* 4:101–3) is surely wrong when he contends that Ramsay's huge popular success with *The Gentle Shepherd* had the effect of emphasizing "the poverty of Scots" as a literary language "unsuited to the complexities of modern communication," and that he passed it on to Burns "as a medium fit only for the crudest of emotional expression." The contrary of this view is certainly closer to the truth. By daring to write what is basically a serious play in (mostly) Scots, Ramsay did not limit the possibilities of the language; rather he opened up opportunities for more subtle exploitation of Scots in the later work of Fergusson, Burns, Sir Walter Scott, R. L. Stevenson, and, in our own time, Hugh MacDiarmid. When Ramsay began to produce Scots poetry about 1712 such possibilities were undreamed of. His success, especially with *The Gentle Shepherd,* proved that something of real literary value could still be done in that language, that Scots was rich and flexible enough even for "modern communication" (whatever that may mean).

The tremendous popularity of the play among all classes was, as Thomas Crawford ably demonstrates,[20] partly a result of the fact that it touches upon most of the central issues in Scottish society in Ramsay's era and later—such matters as agricultural conditions and the relations between lairds and tenants, the education of the folk to overcome superstition and backwardness, the orthodox moralities of love and marriage in the context of a rigid class system, the threat to Scotland's cultural integrity by foreign influences, and so forth. By dealing discreetly with all of these questions Ramsay interested all and offended few. Above all, he rescued Scots from oblivion as a literary language, and assured its future. By fusing the conventions of pastoral with those of sentimental comedy (both derived mainly from contemporary English poetry), with the revolutionary addition of fresh Scottish setting, characters, and poetic language, Ramsay created in *The Gentle Shepherd* his master work as an original poet and assured his permanent place in the history of Scottish, and British, literature.

Summary

The significance of Ramsay's Scots pastorals can be readily summed up under two headings: their historical importance, and their intrinsic value as works of art.

Historically speaking, Ramsay's work in this genre—pastoral elegies, love eclogues, and drama—represents a crucial breakthrough in the evolution of Scottish poetry. Beginning with "Richy and Sandy" in 1719, as we have seen, Ramsay produced in these poems the first poetry in Scots on serious subjects in the modern era, the first since the golden age of the medieval makars. In daring to do so, successfully, he opened up new vistas for the use of Scots as a poetic language for the eighteenth century and beyond. *The Gentle Shepherd,* as a major work, was especially important in this perspective.

Secondly, in these poems Ramsay laid down the foundation for modern Scottish pastoralism. He demonstrated that Scots was in some senses an ideal language for the delineation of the beauty and dignity of rural life. In so doing, he made possible the fine realistic pastorals of Fergusson (especially "The Farmer's Ingle"), and, above all, the powerful and sensitive re-creations of farm and village life in the poetry of Burns.

Though Ramsay's Scots pastorals have a large importance in the historic evolution of Scottish poetry, they are uneven in artistic quality. Of his pastoral elegies, the first two, on Addison and Mary Keith, are relatively weak; but those on Prior and Gay are surprisingly effective. In the love eclogues—"Patie and Roger," "Patie and Pegie," and "Jenny and Meggy"—Ramsay's touch is generally surer; and in "Patie and Roger" especially, which later became the opening scene of his pastoral comedy, Ramsay produced what may well be judged the finest sustained piece of Scots verse in all of his writings. Finally, we come to *The Gentle Shepherd* itself. The plot is slender and relatively trite, as many have pointed out; but in the genre of pastoral drama— by definition an artificial form—one should hardly expect a brilliantly original structure, penetrating psychological insights, or fully developed characters. The same is true of the tradition of sentimental comedy to which it is also related. Within the constrictions of the genre itself Ramsay manages to achieve an unusual freshness, to infuse a breath of Scottish country air into a stale literary mode. *The Gentle Shepherd,* with all its defects, remains a pleasant, interesting, and readable work. It represents, as Crawford says, "a completely new voice in British poetry."[21]

Chapter Five

Scots Songs

Allan Ramsay's very important contributions in the field of Scots song fall into two categories: his work as a collector, anthologist, and publicist of native Scottish songs (a subject that will be taken up in chapter 8); and his achievement as an original writer of Scots words to traditional Scots tunes, which is our concern here. An initial difficulty arises: just how is "Scots song" to be defined? Thomas Crawford in *Society and the Lyric* has convincingly demonstrated that Scots song in the eighteenth century was not a clearly separate art form, but rather a part of a wider *British* song culture; that is to say that Scots songs circulated freely in England and Ireland, just as English and Irish songs were known and popular in Scotland. That does not mean, however, that Scots song has no identity of its own. Scots song surely has special qualities of sadness, sweetness, gaiety, tempo, and tone that distinguish it, though in a very general way, from the English or Irish popular song tradition, with much overlapping. Anyone who has paid attention to the songs of all three cultures will agree that there are definite, though subtle, differences.

Another complicating factor is that in Scotland, as in any culture, a song consists of two disparate elements—music and words. Ramsay as a "composer" was, like Burns, exclusively a wordsmith. He worked mostly, though not exclusively, with traditional Scottish tunes, for which (again like Burns) he provided new or "improved" lyrics, often genteel or arty words to make the "auld sangs" respectable or appropriate for singing by aristocratic Scottish ladies. In the following discussion only those songs that seem to be entirely or mostly Ramsay's (another problem) and that contain at least a tincture of Scots vocabulary will be considered—those in a purely standard English are touched upon later. Ramsay's Scots songs may be treated, more or less chronologically according to dates of publication, under three headings: comic songs printed in *Poems* (1721 and 1728) and in *The Tea-Table Miscellany* (1723–29), serious songs from the same sources, and songs added to *The Gentle Shepherd* in 1728. Ramsay's method of songwriting is generally clear. Like Burns, he always started with the music, usually a traditional Scots tune, though he occasionally used English ones as well; and sometimes he had old words, or fragments of traditional lyrics to work from. At one extreme, whether he knew the old words or not, Ramsay would create a wholly original set of lyrics for the tune—sometimes in English neoclassical poetic diction, as in "The Kind Reception" (*STS*, 1:45–46), his appallingly artificial version of "Auld Lang Syne"; sometimes in his own braid Scots vernacular; and sometimes in a linguistic mixture of the two idioms. At the other extreme, he would on occasion simply refurbish a traditional song, retaining the chorus and part of the old words, while adding some original stanzas and other touches of his own, as in "Jenny Nettles" (*STS*, 3:62). Again as with Burns, there is often a problem in knowing exactly how much of a song is actually by Ramsay; but we can only assume in uncertain cases that a song he attributed to himself by printing it in either of his two volumes of *Poems,* or credited to himself in *The Tea-Table Miscellany,* is substantially his.

Comic Songs in *Poems* and *The Tea-Table Miscellany*

Generally speaking, Ramsay's comic songs in Scots are superior to his serious lyrics, since in the comic ones he was less apt to be tempted into prettifying his language. Let us look first at the handful of Scots songs of a humorous kind which Ramsay produced in the earliest phase of his career and published in *Poems,* 1721.

"Bessy Bell and Mary Gray" (*STS*, 1:49–50), first published in 1720, is quite a good song, with breezy charm and a lively, colloquial style. Its opening stanza reads as follows:

> *O Bessy Bell* and *Mary Gray*
> They are twa bonny lasses,
> They bigg'd a Bower on yon Burn-brae   *built; brookside*
> And theek'd it o'er wi' Rashes.   *thatched; rushes*

> Fair Bessy Bell I loo'd yestreen,   *loved last night*
> And thought I ne'er cou'd alter;
> But *Mary Gray*'s twa pawky Een,   *bewitching eyes*
> They gar my Fancy falter.   *make*

This is a fine beginning, although, as Crawford points out,[1] there are in stanzas 2 and 3 a couple of awkward classical allusions that are not well integrated into the Scots texture. One of these, however, "When *Phoebus* starts frae *Thetis'* lap" (line 11), has the distinction of having inspired a memorable line in Robert Fergusson's "Hallow-fair"—"Whan *Phoebus* ligs [lies] in *Thetis* lap" (line 73).[2] Ramsay's allusion does not work well because he uses it in a "straight" context; Fergusson's is witty and effective because he intends it ironically, and that makes all the difference. Nevertheless, Ramsay's song, on the whole, is fresh and amusing.

Somewhat surer in technique are "The Young Laird and Edinburgh Katy" and its companion piece, "Katy's Answer" (*STS,* 1:51–52). In the former, after a solid introductory stanza, occur two especially excellent lines (9–10):

> O *Katy* wiltu gang wi' me,   *wilt thou go*
> And leave the dinsome Town a while. . . .   *noisy*

Here the importunate desire of the male lover is expressed in the natural rhythms of living speech, but raised to the level of art by Ramsay's choice of the word "dinsome." This adjective is exactly right in the context: it is sufficiently colloquial to blend well with the rest, yet is distinctive and therefore memorable. The effect is comparable to that of Burns's use of "trysted" in the opening lines of "Mary Morison" ("O Mary, at thy window be, / It is the wish'd, the trysted hour").[3] Ramsay's lines have a perfect matching of sound, rhythm, and meaning, a special magic that is rare in his work.

After this high point, "The Young Laird and Edinburgh Katy" in its middle stanzas settles into a pastoralism that is slightly artificial but not excessively so. The final stanza is especially pleasing:

> There's up into a pleasant Glen,
> A wee Piece frae my Father's Tower,   *small distance*

A canny, saft, and flowry Den,   *comfortable*
Which circling Birks has form'd a Bower: *birches*
When e'er the Sun grows high and warm,
We'll to the cauller Shade remove,   *cool*
There will I lock thee in mine Arm,
And love and kiss, and kiss and love.

Altogether, the song is smoothly and skillfully written. In its sequel, "Katy's Answer," Ramsay works in a wholly different tune and rhythm, and he uses a broader Scots with a wittier tone. Here is part of Katy's commonsense response to the urgings of her lover (stanza 2):

Right fain wad I take ye'r Offer,
Sweet Sir, but I'll tine my Tocher,   *lose; dowry*
Then *Sandy* ye'll fret,
And wyt ye'r poor *Kate*,   *blame*
When e'er ye keek in your toom Coffer.   *look; empty*

"Katy's Answer" is one of Ramsay's earliest experiments with the kind of song in which the speaker is female, where he has to project his imagination into the mind and feelings of a woman. Here he manages this persona device with liveliness and wit; in another song of slightly later date, "Polwart on the Green" (*STS,* 1:171–72), he develops the method still further. In "Polwart" the speaker is a girl who offers a rendezvous with a loved lad in an amusingly frank and fresh style, ending as follows:

At *Polwart* on the Green,
Among the new mawn Hay,   *mown*
With Sangs and Dancing keen
We'll pass the heartsome Day,   *cheerful*
At Night if Beds be o'er thrang laid,   *crowded*
And thou be twin'd of thine,   *deprived of*
Thou shalt be welcome, my dear Lad,
To take a Part of mine.

Ramsay's success with the female persona here looks forward to the many songs of Burns—"Last May a Braw Wooer" or "I'm o'er young to Marry Yet,"[4] for example—in which the speaker is a woman.

Among other early songs in Scots in the humorous style, the lilting "O'er Bogie" (*STS*, 1:168–69) deserves mention. But the best of them all, by general agreement, is the splendid drinking song, "Up in the Air" (*STS*, 1:174–75). Daiches calls this one "a real masterpiece," and Crawford gives it a full, laudatory analysis.[5] One of the unexpected delights is the fact that we become aware only gradually that it *is* a drinking song, as Crawford points out. The opening stanza deals with supernatural folklore:

> Now the Sun's gane out o'Sight,
> Beet the Ingle, and snuff the Light: *kindle the fire*
> In Glens the Fairies skip and dance,
> And Witches wallop o'er to France,
>   Up in the Air
>   On my bonny grey Mare.
> And I see her yet, and I see her yet,
>   Up in, &c.

That the witches are a drunken hallucination becomes clearer when we hear in stanza 2 that "The Man i' the Moon / Is carowsing aboon [above], / D'ye see, d'ye see, d'ye see him yet." Finally, in the third stanza, we make the joyful discovery that it is drinking glasses rather than witches that are really "Up in the Air," and the song ends in stanza 4 on a note of roaring conviviality:

> STEEK the Doors, keep out the Frost,   *close*
> Come *Willy* gi'es about ye'r Tost,   *give us; toast*
> Til't Lads, and lilt it out,   *to it*
> And let us ha'e a blythsom Bowt,   *have; bout*
>   Up wi't there, there,
>   Dinna cheat, but drink fair,   *do not*
> Huzza, Huzza, and Huzza Lads yet,
>   Up wi't &c.

This is an excellent song of its kind, with vibrant Scots images and lively, imaginative refrains. In this rollicking lyric Ramsay surpassed himself.

After the publication of *Poems,* 1721, Ramsay continued to compose Scots songs, both comic and serious, for the next seven or eight years with increasing facility. Over a dozen of these he chose to print in his second volume of *Poems* (1728), but many more found places in the four volumes of his *Tea-Table Miscellany.* Of the comic songs published in the 1728 collection, three or four are notable.

"The Bob of Dunblane" (*STS*, 2:77–78) is an amusing colloquial love song in which the speaker is a young man wooing a girl with the well-worn argument of *carpe diem.* Ramsay uses the traditional Scots tune of the same name, and he incorporates the old folk words in his first two lines; the rest of the song seems to be his, and it is quite effective, better, for a change, than Burns's lyrics for this tune.[6] The phrase "Bob of Dunblane" is a double entendre: it signifies both the dance connected with the town of Dunblane in Perthshire, and the act of sexual lovemaking. The opening four lines will illustrate the breezy flavor of Ramsay's song:

Lassie, lend me your braw Hemp Heckle, *flax-comb*
And Ill lend you my Thripling Kame; *rippling comb*
For Fainness, Deary, I'll gar you keckle, *make; cackle*
If ye'll go dance the *Bob of Dunblane.*

Another humorous song of this mildly bawdy kind is "The Highland Laddie" (*STS*, 2:81–82), in which the speaker is a girl; it anticipates in a general way Burns's rousing song by the female pickpocket in "The Jolly Beggars."[7] The penultimate stanza is typical:

Few Compliments between us pass,
I ca' him my dear Highland Laddie: *call*
And he ca's me his Lawland Lass: *Lowland*
Syne rows me in his Highland Plaidy. *then rolls*

The catchy rhymes here, and throughout, help to make this an attractive song.

Better still is "The Widow" (*STS*, 2:287–88), a fast-moving song of courtship advice that fairly gallops along, as the opening stanza will show:

The Widow can bake, and the Widow
    can brew,
The Widow can shape, and the Widow
    can shew,   *sew*
And mony braw Things the Widow can do;   *fine*
    Then have at the Widow, my Laddie.
With Courage attack her baith early   *both*
    and late,
To kiss her and clap her ye   *hug;*
    mauna be blate: *must not be shy*
Speak well, and do better; for that's
    the best Gate   *way*
    To win a young Widow, my Laddie.

This song has a genuine folk quality about it. Ramsay may, in fact, have had some traditional words to build upon, though perhaps only the first line and the general rhythmical pattern. At any rate, he does a beautiful job with the swift anapestic meter wedded to a vigorous, but not too earthy, Scots style. Ramsay maintains a fine artistic balance and unity in this lyric, and, although "The Widow" is not widely known today, it deserves to be recognized as a first-rate comic song, one of Ramsay's very best in this genre.

Of the many comic songs of his in Scots that Ramsay published in *The Tea-Table Miscellany* alone, and did not reprint in his 1728 volume of *Poems* (as he did with "The Bob of Dunblane," "The Highland Laddie," "The Widow," and one or two others), only a few need concern us. "The Cordial" (*STS,* 3:40–41), a moderately bawdy piece that is no more than competent in style, is notable chiefly for its influence on two of Burns's songs. Ramsay's line 8, spoken by the young lass who is frightened by the idea of sleeping with a man, "I'm fleed [scared] he keep me waking," clearly suggested Burns's line 4 in "I'm o'er young to Marry Yet"—"I'm fley'd it make me irie, Sir." Similarly, Ramsay's line 15, "Will ye tent me when I cry" crops up almost verbatim as "O Wha will tent me when I cry" in line 2 of Burns's "The rantin dog the Daddie o't."[8] Apart from its remarkable impact on Burns, "The Cordial" is undistinguished. The same is true of "Steer her up, and had her gawn" (*STS,* 3:46), a mediocre drinking song on the theme that drink is

better than love. Ramsay here uses traditional words for his
first four lines, as does Burns in his song of the same name;
the rest of Burns's lyric is different from Ramsay's and much
superior.[9]

Next come "Clout the Caldron" (hammer the pot) and "The
Malt-Man," two Scots songs on the humorous folk theme of
the visiting repairman or salesman. In "Clout the Caldron" (STS,
3:46–47) Ramsay uses a traditional tune with sexual associations;
again, he incorporates the old words in his first four lines, but
the rest of it seems to be his, and is an example of what Daiches
rightly calls a "skilful, unspoiled re-working of a folk-song."[10]
It became, as many critics have noted, a model for the song
of the Caird (tinker) in Burns's "The Jolly Beggars," though
Burns's version is more of a trade song with fewer sexual
innuendoes.[11] What has not been recognized is that the final
stanza of Ramsay's lyric, in which the woman speaks, bears a
general similarity to a piece called "Wad ye do that?" in Burns's
collection of bawdy Scots songs, The Merry Muses of Caledonia.[12]
At any rate, Ramsay's song is a lively one, full of double enten-
dres. In the opening stanza the wandering tinker boldly offers
his services, both mechanical and sexual: "Gar tell the lady of
the place, / I'm come to clout her caldron." At the end the
lady replies that she has no need of this special expertise, and
she sends him away:

> For there is neither pot nor pan
>   Of mine you'll drive a nail in.
> Then bind your budget on your back,   *leather bag*
>   And nails up in your apron,
> For I've a tinkler under tack   *contract*
>   That's us'd to clout my caldron.

"The Malt-Man" (STS, 3:48) is very similar and equally good,
though here the woman, a hostler wife (tavern keeper), is wholly
compliant. The malt man arrives, in the first stanza, with an
overdue bill which the wife promptly pays off with sexual favors:

> The malt-man comes on *Munday,*
>   He craves wonder sair,   *very sorely*
> Cries, *dame, come gi'e me my siller,*   *silver (money)*
>   *Or malt ye sall ne'er get mair.*   *shall; more*

> I took him into the pantry,
>   And gave him some good
>   cock-broo,   *chicken broth*
>   Syne paid him upon a gantree,   *then; barrell rack*
>   As hostler wives should do.

The rest of the song develops this idea with verve and with equally witty images; it is one of Ramsay's most effective comic lyrics.

At this point three others of Ramsay's humorous Scots songs deserve honorable mention. In "The young Lass contra auld Man" (*STS*, 3:51–52) a girl is the speaker, rejecting a rich old man in the liveliest terms. The song is in four eight-line stanzas, with an excellent refrain coming, unexpectedly, in lines 5 and 6 of each:

> Howt awa I winna hae him!   *fy! away! I will not*
>   Na forsooth I winna hae him!   *in truth*

This sparkling refrain may be traditional, but the bulk of the song, in vigorous braid Scots, is surely Ramsay's.[13] "Song To the Tune of, Jenny beguil'd the Webster" (*STS*, 3:53–54) is equally spirited and also has a young lass as the main speaker. In this instance Ramsay identifies the refrain as "The auld Chorus"; it and Ramsay's opening quatrain read as follows:

> *Up Stairs, down Stairs,*
> *   Timber Stairs fear me.*   *frighten*
> *I'm laith to lie a' Night my lane* *loath; alone*
> *   And Johny's bed sae near me.*

> O Mither dear, I 'gin to fear,   *begin*
>   Tho' I'm baith good and bony,   *both; pretty*
> I winna keep; for in my Sleep   *will not*
>   I start and dream of Johny.

This song, too, is in rich colloquial Scots, with Ramsay's female persona expressing herself with a fresh charm and utter convincingness. Artistically the result is a small triumph.

Another successful song in a different pattern is "The Auld Man's Best Argument" (*STS*, 3:57–85). It is based on an ancient motif and provided part of the inspiration for Burns's "Wha is that at my bower door?"[14] In Ramsay's version a wealthy old man knocks on the door of a young widow at night ("O Wha's that at my Chamber Door?"). Through the first two stanzas she rejects him with scorn and derision, but in the last one he puts forward his most persuasive argument:

> "Then Widow, let these Guineas speak,   *gold coins*
>   "That powerfully plead clinkan,   *clinking*
> "And if they fail, my Mouth I'll steek,   *shut*
>   "And nae mair Love will think on."   *more*
> These court indeed, I maun confess,   *must*
>   I think they make you young, Sir,
> And ten times better can express
>   Affection, than your Tongue, Sir.

Ramsay's nimble use of feminine rhymes here creates an irresistibly light and witty conclusion.

We come, finally, to two masterly songs: "Jenny Nettles" and "The Cock Laird." With the former (*STS*, 3:62) there is a problem as to just how much of the text is original with Ramsay, a question on which the experts are divided.[15] Certainly the tune is old, and some of the words may be also. The probability is that Ramsay, working from traditional fragments, refurbished or rewrote a good part of the lyrics as we now have them. In any event, the song is a fine one, as the opening stanza will show:

> SAW ye *Jenny Nettles,*
>   *Jenny Nettles, Jenny Nettles,*
> Saw ye *Jenny Nettles*
>   Coming frae the Market;
> Bag and Baggage on her Back,
>   Her Fee and Bountith in her Lap;   *servant's extra wages*
> Bag and Baggage on her Back,
>   And a Babie in her Oxter.   *armpit*

We learn in the next stanza that Jenny Nettles's bastard child is by *"Robin Rattle"* who has fled. But Jenny is not the kind of girl to accept the situation meekly; she has taken her fate into her own hands, has quit her job, and is now searching for Robin "To stap it [the baby] in his Oxter." The song is vivacious in its rhythms, solidly Scots in language—a very attractive lyric.

In "The Cock Laird" (*STS,* 3:65–66) Ramsay sets up a humorous dialogue between lovers: the man, a small landowner, is relatively poor and penurious; his sweetheart is a big spender. The laird begins his wooing as follows:

A Cock Laird fou cadgie,	*full amorous*
With *Jenny* did meet,	
He haws'd her, he kiss'd her	*hugged*
And ca'd her his Sweet,	*called*
Wilt thou gae alang	*go*
Wi' me, Jenny, Jenny?	
Thou'se be my ain Lemmane,	*own sweetheart*
Jo *Jenny,* quoth he.	*dear*

Jenny agrees, provided that the laird will supply her with various luxuries in food and fashionable dress. When he protests that his small estate cannot afford such things, she responds with the typical prodigal's solution—he can always buy on credit:

The Borrowstoun Merchants	*city*
Will sell ye on tick,	*credit*
For we man hae braw Things,	*must have*
Abiet they soud break. . . .	*albeit; should*

Crawford judges "The Cock Laird" to be "one of Ramsay's very best songs."[16] Certainly it is one of his liveliest and most enjoyable.

Ramsay produced many more comic songs in Scots, but those discussed above are the most interesting and significant specimens of his work in this vein.

Serious Songs in *Poems* and *The Tea-Table Miscellany*

The tunes for which Ramsay composed serious Scots lyrics are numerous, but the results are, on the average, inferior to what he achieved in the comic style. The basic problem in Ramsay's serious Scots songs is that in them he was too often tempted to slide into varying degrees of English "poetic" diction in order to attain a kind of spurious dignity. The divided culture of Lowland Scotland in the eighteenth century made this stylistic dichotomy almost inevitable, and Ramsay could never fully solve the dilemma, as we have seen in *The Gentle Shepherd* and elsewhere. Burns, too, struggled with the same difficulty in his songcraft sixty years later, though he, on occasion, found ways to write serious and powerful songs in a more or less pure Scots idiom. Ramsay never did. Most often in his serious songs Ramsay resorted to a very diluted Scoto-English diction, or, even worse, to an unhappy mixture of vernacular Scots with prettified English neoclassical poetic formulas. Nevertheless, among the dozens of such songs that he composed, Ramsay managed to reach a level of genuine distinction in three or four, and to strike momentary sparks in a handful of others.

His earliest significant Scots song of this kind is "I'll never leave Thee" (*STS,* 1:170–71), which he published in *Poems* (1721). Written in the form of a dialogue between "Johnny" and "Nelly," this is a competent piece with a rather effective refrain device, though it is weakened by trite sentimentalism and some obtrusive English poetics. The last stanza, however, with its concrete images, is quite good:

Bid Iceshogles hammer red Gauds	*icicles; bars;*
on the Study,	*anvil*
And fair Simmer Mornings nae mair appear	
ruddy;	
Bid *Britons* think ae Gate, and when they	*one way*
obey ye,	
But never till that Time, believe I'll betray ye:	
Leave thee, leave thee, I'll never leave thee;	
The Starns shall gang withershins	*stars; go askew*
e'er I deceive thee.	

In the early 1720s Ramsay composed several more love songs in Scots of this general type. Of these, "Bonny Christy" (*STS,* 2:74–75) and "There's my Thumb I'll ne'er beguile Thee" (*STS,* 2:80–81) are weak and wholly artificial in style. "The bonny

Scot" (*STS*, 2:75–76) is slightly more successful, with a female speaker hoping for the return of her lover, despite parental opposition:

> Ye Gales that gently wave the Sea
> And please the canny Boat-man,   *careful*
> Bear me frae hence, or bring to me
> My brave, my bonny *Scot*-Man.

This is fairly pleasing, though hardly exciting. The refrain using the word "man" was picked up by Burns in "The Ronalds of the Bennals," "Elegy on Captain Matthew Henderson," and other poems.[17]

In "Ann [if] thou were my ain Thing" (*STS*, 2:79–80) there is a definite improvement in technique. Ramsay adopts the fine traditional refrain for this tune, but the rest appears to be wholly his own. Here is the refrain and the second stanza:

> Ann thou were my ain Thing,   *if; own*
> I would love thee, I would love thee;
> Ann thou were my ain Thing,
> How dearly would I love thee.
>
> Sae lang's I had the Use of Light,
> I'd on thy Beauties feast my Sight,
> Syne in saft Whispers through the Night,   *then*
> I'd tell how much I loo'd thee.   *loved*

Apart from occasional labored images, such as the trite "feasting on beauties" formula, Ramsay's style here is straightforward and pleasing.

With "A Song. Tune of Lochaber no more" (*STS*, 2:281–82), first published in *The Tea-Table Miscellany*, volume 2 (1726), Ramsay reached the peak of his form as a writer of serious Scots songs. This one is often found in anthologies; it is, in fact, among the two or three most widely known of all Ramsay's songs, and it deserves to be. Written in Ramsay's genteel Scoto-English idiom, "Lochaber no more" is exceptional in the perfect integration of its style; it has no jarring flaws or artistic blunders, as the famous opening stanza shows:

> Farewell to *Lochaber,* and farewell, my *Jean,*
> Where heartsome with thee I've mony Day been;
> For *Lochaber* no more, *Lochaber* no more,
> We'll may be return to *Lochaber* no more.
> These Tears that I shed, they are a' for my Dear,
> And no for the Dangers attending on Weir,   *war*
> Tho' bore on rough Seas to a far bloody Shore,
> May be to return to *Lochaber* no more.

This is Ramsay's serious lyric verse at its best. The light infusion of Scots words or spellings, blending unobtrusively with the sonorous generalities, the beautiful impact of the repeated phrase "Lochaber no more"—all work to intensify the emotional force of the song and to create just the right effect of sad sweetness.[18] The end result is a very good song indeed.

Another Scots love song on the same separation-by-war theme is "The Soger Laddie" (*STS,* 2:290), though in this case the woman is the speaker. She begins as follows:

> My Soger laddie is over the Sea,   *soldier*
> And he will bring Gold and Money to me;
> And when he comes hame, he'll make me a Lady: *home*
> My Blessing gang with my Soger Laddie.   *go*

The tone here, obviously, is much lighter than in "Lochaber no more," with some hackneyed phrasing and a weaker emotional effect, but the song has brisk rhythms and tempo which make it attractive. Much less successful aesthetically is "A Scots Cantata," (*STS,* 3:36–37), consisting of two narrative sections or "Recitatives" in pentameter quatrains (*a b a b*), and two "Airs" in the "Christis Kirk" stanza without the tag-line (*a b a b c d c d*). The whole suffers from lack of artistic unity: the braid Scots phrases clash agonizingly with conventional poetic formulas. This mediocre performance, nevertheless, has historical significance. For one thing, the cantata probably served as a kind of warm up for the operatic version of *The Gentle Shepherd.* More importantly, it surely provided Burns with the idea for the form of his infinitely greater cantata, "The Jolly Beggars."[19]

Much more interesting in itself is "This is not mine ain House" (*STS,* 3:43–44), Ramsay's deft rewriting of a folk song. In this instance one would guess from the style that only the first two lines are "old words," the remainder being original with Ramsay. The speaker is a newly married bride, looking forward to leaving her father's house and moving into her husband's. In the last of three stanzas the song degenerates somewhat as Ramsay puts into the girl's mouth some extremely conventional marriage moralities and the idea that the woman's place is in the home—a touch of male chauvinism that sounds unnatural in our time, especially coming from a woman, but that doubtless seemed quite normal in Ramsay's generation. At any rate, the opening of the song is very fine:

> This is not mine ain house,
> I ken by the rigging o't; *know; of it*
> Since with my love I've changed vows,
> I dinna like the bigging o't. *construction*
> For now that I'm young *Robie's* bride,
> And mistress of his fire-side,
> Mine ain house I'll like to guide,
> And please me with the trigging o't. *trimming*

The frank and eager anticipation of the bride is skillfully suggested here, and the song as a whole has an unspoiled folksy charm.

"The Highland Lassie" (*STS*, 3:56–57), which also incorporates folk materials, is equally effective. The speaker, a highlander, prefers his lass, even though she is poor, above the wealthy, pampered girls of the Lowland cities (stanza 2):

> Than ony Lass in Borrowstoun, *the city*
> Wha mak their Cheeks with Patches motie, *spotty*
> I'd tak my *Katie* but a Gown, *without*
> Bare footed in her little Cotie. *coat*

Most of the song maintains this lively colloquial style which gives it a pleasing distinction.

We come, finally, to "For the Sake of Some-body" (*STS*, 3:62–64), another good Scots love song in a semiserious style. The refrain in this one is probably traditional, and goes as follows:

> For the Sake of Some-body,
> For the Sake of Some-body;
> I cou'd wake a Winter Night,
> For the Sake of Some-body.

Burns's song of the same title is based on Ramsay's and, for a change, is clearly inferior to its model. In later years the song became associated with the Jacobite rebellion of 1745, and "Some-body" became a not-so-secret name for Bonny Prince Charlie, as it is in Burns's lyric.[20] The main body of Ramsay's song consists of three eight-line stanzas set up as a courting dialogue between a lad and his lass. The middle section, spoken by the girl, will illustrate the flavor of the whole:

Bony Lad, I carena by,	*don't care*
Tho' I try my Luck with thee,	
Since ye are content to tye	
The *Haff-mark* Bridal Band wi' me;	*private marriage*
I'll slip hame and wash my Feet,	
And steal on Linnings fair and clean,	*linens*
Syne at the trysting Place we'll meet,	*then*
To do but what my Dame has done.	

It should be noted, incidentally, that Ramsay manages to get an approximate rhyme here with "clean" and "done," given the Scots pronunciation of "done" as "din"; as was his habit Ramsay anglicizes his spelling to avoid confusing his readers with a purely phonetic rendering. Daiches accurately characterizes "For the Sake of Some-body" as "a fine lilting piece in true folk-style."[21] It is one of Ramsay's most skillful efforts in the genre of Scots song.

Songs Added to *The Gentle Shepherd*

Late in the year 1728, as we have seen, Ramsay converted *The Gentle Shepherd* into a ballad opera through the insertion of seventeen new songs interspersed through the play, in addition to the four songs in the original version. He did this at the urging of the students in Haddington Grammar School who had seen a performance of Gay's *Beggar's Opera* and been excited by it. The transformed pastoral comedy was given a musical performance in Edinburgh in January 1729, and later in the same year Ramsay printed the new songs in *The Tea-Table Miscellany.* According to the manuscript "Life" (*STS,* 4:72–73), he soon regretted having succumbed in this way to the popular craze for ballad opera: "He did not reflect, at the time, that the Beggar's Opera was only meant as a piece of ironical satire, whereas his Gentle Shepherd was a simple imitation of Nature, and neither a mimicry or mockery of any other performance. He was soon, however, sensible of his error, and would have been glad to have retracted those songs. But it was too late."

Ramsay may, however, have had another reason for regret: the new songs that he composed for this purpose, no doubt hastily, are on the whole disappointing in artistic quality, and their author probably sensed this. Nearly all of them are set to beautiful Scottish folk tunes, but Ramsay's lyrics tend to be sententious and artificial. Of the seventeen only two or three rise above mediocrity.

The best of them all is the very first song, sung by Patie to open the operatic version. Set to the traditional tune of "The wawking of the Faulds," it begins as follows (*STS,* 3:67–68):

> My *Peggy* is a young thing,
>   Just enter'd in her teens,
> Fair as the day, and sweet as May,
> Fair as the day, and always gay.
>   My Peggy is a young thing,
>   And I'm not very auld,   *old*
>   Yet well I like to meet her at
>   The wawking of the fauld.   *watching; fold*

This is a fine, spritely song of youth and love. Using a modest tincture of Scots diction, Ramsay strikes here a delicate balance of the conventional "literary" and the "hamely" styles. It is one of the best of his genteel love songs, and is expertly crafted to introduce *The Gentle Shepherd,* to create just the right atmosphere of pastoral freshness and innocence.

In this operatic version of his play Ramsay numbers his songs, just as Gay does in *The Beggar's Opera.* "Sang II" (*STS,* 3:68) is a fair effort in the faintest of Scoto-English. "Sang III" (*STS,*

3:68–69), to the tune of "Polwart on the Green," is in pure
Scots but is far too contrived for its context. Sung by Peggy
to Jenny in act 1, scene 2, it begins, "The dorty [overly proud]
will repent," and involves a labored comparison between the
woman who is too coy with men and the pampered child
("dawted Bairn") who will not eat its dinner. It reminds one
of some of the songs in *The Beggar's Opera* where Gay uses
outrageous images for comic or ironic effects. By introducing
that kind of figure here, in a serious debate between Peggy
and Jenny, Ramsay achieves only a strained awkwardness, and
the song (though it is in language the most *Scottish* of them
all) is an artistic failure.

The next several songs are generally mediocre, until we come
to "Sang X," a rather charming duet between Peggy and Patie
in act 2, scene 4 (*STS,* 3:71–72). Peggy begins:

When first my dear laddie gade to the green hill,	*went*
And I at ew-milking first seyd my young skill,	*tried*
To bear the milk-bowie, nae pain was to me,	*pail*
When I at the bughting foregather'd with thee.	*milking*

The duet, on the whole, is perhaps too conventionally "pastoral," but it has its moments with some attractive concrete details
that give it a modest distinction. "Sang XVIII," wholly in standard English, rather abstract in imagery, and sentimental in tone,
nevertheless has a degree of vitality and charm.

The rest of the songs added to *The Gentle Shepherd* are competent but generally undistinguished. One of them, however, is
notable for its effect on Burns. "Sang XIX" (*STS,* 3:77), sung
by Peggy to the tune of "Bush aboon Traquair" in act 4, scene
2, is a sentimental love song in English which anticipates Burns's
"I Love my Jean" in overall conception and in some phrasing.[22]
In Ramsay's song Peggy foresees that after Patie's departure
she will remember him in association with various natural scenes
they have known together. The second stanza of Burns's song
is based on a somewhat similar idea, where the speaker asserts
that he "sees" his love in the beauties of nature—"I see her
in the dewy flowers," and so forth. More conclusively, Ramsay's
lines 9 and 10 ("To all our haunts I will repair, / By greenwood-
shaw or fountain") are echoed in Burns's lines 13 and 14
("There's not a bonny flower, that springs / By fountain, shaw,

or green"). This parallel, hitherto unnoticed, is further evidence
of how carefully Burns must have read, and reread, the poems
and songs of Allan Ramsay.

Summary

Ramsay is obviously not a great lyric poet. Moreover, he
had the misfortune to be totally eclipsed in this genre two
generations later by the greatest songwriter of all time in any
language—Robert Burns. In modern times "Scots song" has
come to be almost equated with Burns, and his towering accomplishment has unfairly overshadowed the pioneer work of Ramsay. Yet Ramsay, in many respects, started it all: he saw the
opportunity, he laid the essential foundation, he showed what
could be done. Ramsay's work in Scots song has often been
undervalued, but he deserves credit for a crucial historic achievement: he rescued the genre from the obscurity and fragility
of oral tradition, made it accessible, respectable, and popular
among all classes, and passed it on to Burns.

From an artistic point of view Ramsay's Scots songs are very
uneven in quality. The bulk of them, of course, are mediocre
or worse. But any writer must finally be judged by his finest
work, and Ramsay's best Scots songs are very good indeed.
"Up in the Air," for example, is hard to beat as a drinking
song, and a few others of Ramsay's comic songs in braid Scots
are first-rate, including "The Widow," "Jenny Nettles," "The
Cock Laird," and perhaps "The Bob of Dunblane," "Clout the
Caldron," "The young Lass contra auld Man," and part of "The
Young Laird and Edinburgh Katy." In a more serious vein
Ramsay reached the peak of his abilities less often, but once
in a while he hit upon a near-perfect harmony, as in "Lochaber
no more," "This is not mine ain House," "For the Sake of
Some-body," and, possibly, "My Peggy is a young thing."

In the well over one hundred lyrics that he composed, Ramsay's most common failing is in the jarring disunity of style
and language that ruins many of his songs; but this is true of
Burns also. Occasionally, however, Ramsay succeeded—in some
comic songs in rich vernacular, and in a very few serious ones
in a skillful fusion of Scots and English—and he did so just
often enough to establish Scots songs as a vital and compelling
art form for his century.

Chapter Six
Scots Fables and Tales

In one other area of Scottish poetry, that of narrative verse, Ramsay produced interesting work. In this field his efforts fall into three fairly specialized genres: imitations of older Scots narrative poetry, Scots fables, and comic tales.

Imitations of Older Scots Narrative Poetry

In *The Ever Green* (1724), his ambitious anthology of Middle Scots poetry based mainly on the Bannatyne Manuscript, Ramsay inserted three unacknowledged productions of his own, disguised as older poetry. These are, in ascending order of importance, "The Eagle and Robin Red-breist," a fable in pseudo–Middle Scots; Ramsay's substantial additions to "Hardyknute, A Fragment," a fake ballad actually written by Lady Wardlaw; and "The Vision," Ramsay's extensive patriotic dream-vision poem, again in his imitation of Middle Scots style. It has long been recognized that Ramsay was far from expert in Middle Scots, that from the point of view of modern linguistic study he was an amateur. The fact is that serious scholarly study of Middle Scots did not even begin until the latter part of the eighteenth century, pioneered by men like Lord Hailes and John Pinkerton.[1] Ramsay himself was no scholar, and it should be remembered that in his generation *no one* was expert in the Middle Scots language. Ramsay was a popularizer and propagandist for Middle Scots poetry, and it is surprising that he did so well under the circumstances, both as the author of "fake" medieval poems and as the editor of real ones. He had, however, two redeeming assets: he loved the old poems and read them with loving care, even though he did not understand them in some details; and he was himself a capable, creative poet with a poet's sensitivity to language.

In "The Eagle and Robin Red-breist" (*STS,* 3:95–96) Ramsay

presents a fairly lively fable of an eagle holding court with smaller birds, with perhaps some slight suggestions from Chaucer's *The Parlement of Fowles.* The moral is to beware of the vicious envy of courtiers.[2] A brief passage (lines 5–8) will illustrate Ramsay's style:

This Ryall *Bird,* tho braif and great,	*royal; brave*
And armit strang for stern Debait,	*armed*
Nae Tyrant is but condescends	
Aftymes to treit inferiour Friends.	*oftimes; treat*

To a reader whose ear is tuned to the "feel" of Middle Scots such lines will lack authenticity. For example, the use of the verb "treat" in the sense of "provide an especially luxurious meal for" is clearly modern, not medieval. Ramsay's method in these quasi-medieval poems is simply to write in his own natural eighteenth-century Scots, and then to revise the spellings and some diction to give an antique flavor to the verse. The original manuscript version of this fable (*STS,* 6:113–14) gives indisputable proof of his procedure: in the lines cited above, for example, he changes the manuscript "Royal" to "Ryall," "armd complete" to "armit strang," and so forth. But Ramsay does this with considerable skill here, and the result is pleasing enough. His verse form, as in all of his Scots fables and tales (except for "The Fox and the Rat"), is tetrameter couplets, the traditional Scottish meter for narrative poetry.

In "Hardyknute" (*STS,* 4:282–93) Ramsay goes on to attempt the style of the folk ballad. The irony here is that this ballad is itself a fake; Ramsay may not have recognized it as such, but believed it to be a genuine "fragment." On the other hand, perhaps he knew or suspected its modern origin, and therefore saw it as fair game for his own "additions." In either case, as we now know, "Hardyknute" was written by a Scottish gentlewoman, Lady Wardlaw (1677–1727), and published anonymously by her in 1719 as a real "find." Ramsay not only included it in *The Ever Green* (in a version with more antiquated spelling than Lady Wardlaw had used),[3] but he fleshed it out with thirteen stanzas of his own composition, to make up a total of forty-two eight-line stanzas in the common ballad meter. Stanza 38, one of Ramsay's additions, will illustrate his style:

ON *Norways* Coast the Widowit Dame	*widowed*
May wash the Rocks with Teirs,	*tears*
May lang luke owre the Schiples Seis	*look; shipless seas*
Befoir hir Mate appeirs.	
Ceise, *Emma,* ceise to hope in Vain,	
Thy Lord lyis in the Clay,	*lies*
The valziant SCOTS nae *Revers* thole	*valiant; robbers endure*
To carry Lyfe away.	

We may note here faint echoes of the genuine ballad of "Sir Patrick Spence" ("Lang, lang may their ladies stand," etc.), a ballad that Lady Wardlaw had also borrowed from in stanza 5 ("Drinking the Blude-reid Wyne"). Furthermore, if one reads this stanza, or any of Ramsay's additions, phonetically, ignoring the old fashioned spelling, it becomes clear that in "Hardyknute," as in "The Eagle and Robin Red-breist," Ramsay is actually writing in his own contemporary vernacular; the "antique" quality is imparted by the spelling alone. The same is true of Lady Wardlaw's part of the poem. Nevertheless, Ramsay's imitation is at least as good as hers; he must have been well acquainted with oral poetry, for he approximates the stark mode of the popular ballad with skill and sensitivity.

A much more impressive effort of this kind is "The Vision" (*STS*, 3:81–95), which bears the spurious subtitle *"Compylit in* Latin *be a most lernit Clerk in Tyme of our Hairship* [hardship] *and Oppression,* anno 1300, *and translatit in* 1524." It also has a false ascription at the end—*"Quod* AR. SCOT."—the same one that Ramsay used for "The Eagle and Robin Red-breist." "AR. SCOT." is probably a semitransparent code for "Allan Ramsay, Scotsman," which would have amused those of his friends and readers who were in the know. For his meter Ramsay chose the old Scots form of Alexander Montgomerie's *The Cherrie and the Slae,* a complex fourteen-line stanza that he had experimented with elsewhere[4] and here manages with skill. The date of composition of this work is uncertain, but it was most probably written between 1718, when Ramsay first borrowed the Bannatyne Manuscript and became deeply interested in Middle Scots poetry, and 1724, when he printed the poem in *The Ever Green.*

"The Vision" belongs to the genre of the medieval "dream-vision" poem in which the narrator falls asleep, dreams a dream, and wakens at the end. The most famous example of the type in British literature is, of course, William Langland's monumental *Piers Plowman,* but dozens of other specimens could be cited. Ramsay sets his poem in the 1290s during the reign of John Baliol as puppet king of Scotland for the English monarch Edward I, a time when the Scottish kingdom came temporarily under English control and was therefore comparable to Ramsay's own era after the Union of 1707. "The Vision" is, in fact, like "A Tale of Three Bonnets," a satire on the Union, though subtler and less outspoken than the earlier work.

In the opening stanzas (1–3) we see the narrator taking shelter in "a canny Cave" from stormy weather, in a passage vaguely reminiscent of the introduction to Henryson's *Testament of Cresseid.* He promptly falls asleep and has a vision of a venerable old man who turns out to be the guardian angel of Scotland ("The *Warden* of this auntient Nation"). The description of this august figure (stanzas 4–7) looks forward to Burns's picture of "Coila," the muse of his native Kyle (central Ayrshire) in his poem of the same name; Burns's "The Vision" obviously owes something in a general way to Ramsay's conception.[5] The fifth stanza will exemplify both Ramsay's verse form and his style in this picture of the Warden:

Grit Darring dartit frae his Ee,	*great daring; eye*
A Braid-sword schogled at his	*broadsword shook;*
Thie,	*thigh*
On his left Arm a Targe;	*shield*
A shynand Speir filld his richt Hand,	*shining spear*
Ot stalwart Mak, in Bane and Brawnd,	*likeness; bone; sinew*
Of just Proportions, large;	
A various Rain-bow colourt Plaid	*colored*
Owre his left Spaul he threw,	*shoulder*
Doun his braid Back, frae his quhyt Heid,	*white head*
The Silver Wymplers grew;	*curls*
Amaisit, I gaisit	*amazed; gazed*
To se, led at Command	*see*
A strampant and rampant	
Ferss Lyon in his Hand.	*fierce*

In terms of artistic quality this is an average stanza in "The Vision." Once again, Ramsay is writing basically in his own

eighteenth-century Scots, but in this poem he takes greater pains
than in "The Eagle and Robin Red-breist" to simulate Middle
Scots spelling—"shynand" for "shining," "quhyt" for "white,"
and so forth. There are few crass blunders (none in this stanza),
and for the nonspecialist like Ramsay himself and, indeed, *all*
of his readers, the effect was convincing enough.

Ramsay goes on to use his dream-vision device to bring out
pointed satiric parallels between Baliol's Scotland and his own.
In the last lines of stanza 8, for example, he portrays Scotsmen
chafing under the treasonous deal that Baliol has made with
the English:

Regretand and fretand	*regretting; fretting*
Ay at his cursit Plot,	*always*
Quha rammed and crammed	*who*
That Bargin doun thair throt.	*throat*

Ramsay saw the Union in just those terms, and his language
here has a sharp edge to it. The same is true of several other
passages: as in his reference to "this disgraceful Paction" (line
129), and the Warden's hope that things will change "Quhen
Scottish Peirs slicht [Lords slight] *Saxon* Gold, / And turn trew
heartit Men" (lines 177–78). Ramsay also attacks absentee land-
lords, extravagance, and sycophancy among the ruling class in
lines 313–22 and elsewhere. Despite some strained stanzas (the
nineteenth, for example, describing a drinking party among the
Roman gods, which falls flat), "The Vision" is a hard-hitting
satire on contemporary Scotland. Ramsay's readers could hardly
have failed to make the connections.

As a daring imitation of Middle Scots by an early eighteenth-
century man who was an enthusiastic amateur in the language,
"The Vision" is not to be sneered at.[6] Ramsay's effort was quite
different from the dishonest charlatanism perpetrated later in
the century by James MacPherson in his "Ossianic" poems or
even by Thomas Chatterton in his forgeries of Middle English
verse. Ramsay's intent was not so much to deceive his readers
as to throw a protective coloring over his bold criticism of the
parliamentary Union of 1707. For this purpose, his setting of
the poem in Scotland at the time of Baliol was remarkably effective. Even in the linguistic perspective "The Vision" is not nearly

so bad as has been suggested; it is, in fact, a fairly impressive performance, and has been generally underestimated by the critics.

Scots Fables

Ramsay turned to the writing of fables relatively late in his career. He produced, altogether, some thirty of them, of which twenty are adaptations of the French fables of La Motte, three are based on La Fontaine, and seven seem to be of his own invention.[7] As far as we can tell his work in this genre came mainly in two spurts of composition in 1721–22 and 1728–29. The earlier of his two sets of fables was probably written after the publication of *Poems* (1721), since none of them appeared there, but were issued in a slender separate volume as *Fables and Tales* in 1722. Ramsay was possibly inspired in this effort by an English translation of La Motte that appeared in 1720, and he may have been further encouraged by the publication of the first edition of John Gay's *Fables* in 1722. For the next few years he apparently suspended his activity in this field, with the single exception of the brief "Fable of the Lost Calf" which he printed in the fourth edition of his *Poems* in 1727. In 1728, however, in his second volume of *Poems* Ramsay reprinted all of the items from *Fables and Tales* (1722). Probably as a result of the favorable reception of that collected edition he returned to the genre and composed a second set of fables, which appeared for the first time in 1729.[8]

In his Scots fables based on La Motte and La Fontaine, Ramsay adopted a method similar to that which he had used earlier in his "translations" of the *Odes* of Horace—that is to say, these are not so much translations as very free adaptations of the originals. Kinghorn, in his perceptive discussion of Ramsay's fables (*STS*, 4:121–26), has convincingly demonstrated the differences by placing several passages of Ramsay alongside the corresponding lines in La Motte. The style of La Motte is concise, polished, and pleasingly artificial (the same is true of La Fontaine); that of Ramsay is earthy and exuberant. In some cases Ramsay blithely skips over details in La Motte, but more often he expands upon his source, as in the following passage in "The twa Lizards" (*STS*, 2:48–50). La Motte sets his scene in two

succinct lines: "Au coin d'un bois, le long d'une muraille, /
Deux lézards, bons amis, conversoient au Soleil," of which a
literal version would be: "in the corner of a wood, along a
wall, two lizards, good friends, were talking in the sun." In
Ramsay's version these two lines become four:

Beneath a Tree, ae shining Day,	*one*
On a Burn-bank twa *Lizards* lay	*brookside*
Beeking themsells now in the Beams,	*baking*
Then drinking of the cauller Streams.	*cool*

Ramsay not only expands La Motte's description, but he also
changes several details and adds wholly new images, such as
"cauller Streams," that are nowhere in his source. He tends
to domesticate the French fables in a Scottish landscape, with
a moderate degree of Scots idiom. In general, Ramsay's style
in these fables is less pointed and clever than that of La Motte
or La Fontaine, but it has greater vigor and realism. His Scots
vernacular works very well in imparting a lively, folksy quality
that is lacking in his models.

   On the whole, Ramsay's Scots adaptations of the French fables
make for pleasant reading; his vernacular renderings are often
fresh and surprising, as two or three illustrations will show.
"The Miser and Minos" (*STS*, 2:38–39), also derived from
La Motte, is especially amusing. It begins with a description
of a rich miser, which anticipates Ramsay's own poem, "The
Last Speech of a Wretched Miser" (1724). In this case the heirs
bury the miser in the cheapest possible fashion (lines 13–16):

They'll scarce row up the Wretch's Feet,	*wrap up*
Sae scrimp they make his Winding-sheet,	*so short*
Tho' he shou'd leave a vast Estate,	
And Heaps of Gowd like	*gold;*
Arthur's Seat.	(*hill at Edinburgh*)

At the entrance to hell the miser refuses to pay the boatman
to ferry him across the River Styx; instead, he swims across
himself, and then is brought before the judge Minos to be pun-
ished for this crime. His sin in refusing to pay the fee is so
unheard of that the judge at first is baffled—"The Case was

new, and very kittle [ticklish], / Which puzzl'd a' the Court na little" (lines 37–38). In the end, after rejecting the standard punishments, Minos finds a just solution (lines 50–55).

> Weak are our Punishments below,
> For sic a Crime;—he maun be hurl'd   *such; must*
> Straight back again into the World.
> I sentence him to see and hear,
> What Use his Friends make of his Gear.   *property*

This fable, lively and pointed in its own right, looks even better in Scottish dress.

Among others of Ramsay's adaptations published in 1722, "Jupiter's Lottery" (*STS,* 2:36–38) and "The twa Cats and the Cheese" (*STS,* 2:45–46) are especially well done. Of his later fables, published in 1729, one of the best is "The Fox turn'd Preacher. A Thought" (*STS,* 3:112–13), based on La Motte's "Le Renard Prédicateur." This one is a delightful satire on hypocrisy. An elderly fox ("A Learned Fox grown stiff with Eild"), looking for a meal, adopts the stratagem of disguising himself as an evangelical preacher (lines 7–10):

> He cleath'd himsell in Reverend Dress,   *clothed*
> And turn'd a Preacher.—Nathing less!
> Held forth wi' Birr, 'gainst Wier unjust,   *forcefulness; war*
> 'Gainst Theft and gormondizing Lust.   *gluttonous*

The old fox gathers a large congregation of poultry and sheep to whom he preaches against the practice of killing living creatures for food. He argues that the soul at death leaves the body to inhabit that of another animal, so that in killing animals we may be murdering our near relations—"Thus young Miss Goose may be my Mither" (line 40). After this inspiring and confidence-building sermon, a few of the listeners stay behind to ask questions, and the wily fox moves into action (lines 53–58):

> But after a' the lave was gane,   *rest; gone*
> Some Geese, twa Chickens and a Hen,
> Thought fit to stay a little Space,
> To tawk about some kittle Case.   *talk; difficult*

The Doctor hem'd! and in he drew them,   *coughed*
Then quiet and decently he slew them.

This is Ramsay as Scots fabulist at his amusing best.
In his boisterous, realistic versions of these French fables Ramsay is generally successful. In those of his own invention, on the other hand, he tends to fall rather flat. The problem is that in this genre Ramsay is not particularly gifted in dreaming up new material. With La Motte and La Fontaine he had, by and large, very good stories to begin with, and he made the most of them in his charming Scots idiom. His own original fables are inclined to be trivial or rather pointless in effect because the stories themselves are very thin. This is certainly true of "The Ass and the Brock" (*STS*, 2:41–42), "The Spring and the Syke" (*STS*, 2:53–54), and "The Daft Bargain" (*STS*, 2:54–55). Of the seven fables that appear to be original with Ramsay, only "The twa Cut-Purses" (*STS*, 2:55–56) is really enjoyable. This one involves another kind of confidence game, in which simple rural folk attending a town fair are victimized. It opens as follows:

In Borrows-town there was a Fair,
And mony a Landart Coof was there   *country fool*
Baith Lads and Lasses busked brawly,   *dressed finely*
To glowr at ilka Bonny-waly.   *stare; every toy*

One of a pair of rogues gathers a crowd by standing in the stocks with head and hands through the holes, playing the fool. While the people are distracted by these antics, their pockets are picked by the other cutpurse, who then disappears. When an uproar ensues over the thefts, the fool in the stocks addresses the crowd (lines 31–34):

Said he, my Friends, I'm very sorry
To hear your melancholy Story;
But sure whate'er your Tinsel be,   *losses*
Ye canna lay the Wyte on me.   *blame*

There is a spark of wit in this one, but generally Ramsay's original fables are disappointing and fall far below the artistic level of his adaptations from the French.

Scots Tales

Another narrative genre that Ramsay attempted with considerable success was the Scots tale, or, more precisely, the fabliau. The fabliau, essentially a medieval form that originated in France in the thirteenth and fourteenth centuries, is a humorous short story in verse, usually with lower- or middle-class characters, and always involving some kind of ingenious trick or practical joke. The greatest fabliaux in our literature are the half dozen of Chaucer's in *The Canterbury Tales* (some of which clearly influenced Ramsay). There are also a very few specimens in Middle Scots, including "The Freiris of Berwick" (sometimes attributed to William Dunbar but probably not by him) which was the model for Ramsay's best tale. Altogether, Ramsay produced four tales in Scots of the fabliau type: "The Monk and the Miller's Wife" (published 1724) and its sequel "The Miller and his Man" (composed about 1728), "The Lure" (published 1728), and "The Clever Offcome" (ca. 1728). Of these the last two are of lesser importance and may be treated briefly. All are composed in tetrameter couplets.

"The Lure: A Tale" (*STS*, 2:155–58) is a fairly clever fabliau with an anti-Catholic bias. The opening scene, in which a falconer meets the devil in disguise, owes something in a general way to the beginning of Chaucer's *Friar's Tale* where a summoner encounters a similar tricky fiend. Ramsay's falconer proudly demonstrates to the devil the speed and skill of his hawk who flies and then returns obediently to the falconer's lure. The devil matches this performance by snatching up "a hooded Friar" and flinging him into the air; then, as his lure, he seizes a fresh country lass, turns her upside down, and waves her at the flying friar (lines 107–12):

Her in his Hand slee *Belzie* hint up,	*sly; grabbed*
As eith as ye wad do a Pint-Stoup,	*easily; tankard*
Inverted, wav'd her round his Head:	
Whieu,—whieu,—he whistled, and with Speed	
Down, quick as shooting Starns, the Priest	*stars*
Came souse upon the Lass's Breast.	*falling heavily*

Ramsay refers to the flying cleric as "Friar," "Monk," and "Priest" with careless inconsistency—perhaps to him they were

all equally depraved—and this creates a degree of confusion
that mars the tale. Otherwise, "The Lure," outrageous as it
is, is a moderately skillful and entertaining comic poem.

"The Clever Offcome" (*STS,* 3:210–12) is another fabliau
on the motif of the unfaithful wife who is caught by her husband
but quick-wittedly talks her way out of the situation and con-
vinces him of her innocence. It is based on La Fontaine's tale
of "Le Mari Confesseur," but is far from a servile imitation
or translation; rather, Ramsay builds upon La Fontaine's slender
sketch and fleshes it out with a broad humor of his own. For
some reason Ramsay chose not to publish this tale during his
lifetime, though it is effective and amusing—not as gross as
"The Lure" and at least as funny.

The best of Ramsay's Scots tales is "The Monk and the Miller's
Wife" (*STS,* 2:146–53), originally published in 1724 in a pamphlet with his English poem "Health," and then reprinted in
his collected *Poems* of 1728. In this instance Ramsay used as
his starting point the Middle Scots fabliau of "The Freiris of
Berwick" which he found in the Bannatyne Manuscript. He
transformed the two friars of his model into a single, young
traveling scholar (Ramsay's title is misleading since there is no
"Monk" in his tale), but otherwise he followed the plot outline
of the old poem fairly closely. That he also acknowledged some
debt in a very general way to the fabliaux of Chaucer is shown
by his use of two lines from *The Miller's Tale* as the motto for
his 1724 edition.[9] Ramsay's tale, however, is not a medieval
imitation, but is written in his own eighteenth-century Scots;
he borrowed the plot only—the style and details of imagery
are entirely his own.

The most attractive quality in "The Monk and the Miller's
Wife" is its vigor and swiftness of tempo. Ramsay sets up his
opening situation with remarkable conciseness, for example, in
lines 5–12:

AN honest Miller wond in *Fife,*	lived
That had a young and wanton Wife,	
Wha sometimes thol'd the Parish Priest	allowed
To mak her Man a twa-horn'd Beast:	(*i.e., a cuckold*)
He paid right mony Visits till her;	to
And to keep in with *Hab* the Miller	
He endeavour'd aft to mak him happy,	
Where e'er he kend the Ale was nappy.	knew; strong

Ramsay maintains this brisk, jaunty pace through the entire fabliau.

The plot thickens when a wandering scholar, James, seeking refuge for the night, arrives at Hab's mill. Hab directs him to his house where, he says, his wife will take care of him ("Gae warm ye, and crack [talk] with our Dame") until he (the miller) can get there. James arrives at the house where the wife, of course, is already entertaining the priest. Naturally, the wife does not dare to admit him, but puts him off with a wonderfully apt speech (lines 63–72):

"I dinna ken ye, quoth the Wife,	*don't know*
"And up and down the Thieves are rife:	*plentiful*
"Within my lane, I'm but a Woman;	*by myself*
"Sae I'll unbar my Door to nae Man.	
"But since 'tis very like, my Dow,	*dove (dear)*
"That all ye're telling may be true,	
"Hae there's a Key, gang in your Way	*here; go*
"At the neist Door, there's braw Ait Strae;	*next; oat straw*
"Streek down upon't, my Lad, and learn,	*stretch*
"They're no ill lodg'd that get a Barn."	

There is a bright, natural flow of colloquial language here that is wholly delightful.

Subsequently, through a hole in the wall between barn and cottage James observes the priest making love to the wife, who afterwards sets the table with a fine roasted hen and bottles of ale and beer. As priest and wife are about to eat, her husband suddenly arrives, so that hen, bottles, and priest must all be hidden away before the wife opens the door. Hab then asks about the scholar, and promptly brings James in from the barn. The miller then asks his wife to put on a good meal for their guest, but she replies that they have only ordinary porridge in the house. At this point the scholar confesses that he has magic powers and offers to conjure up something better. He then goes through a phoney hocus pocus routine, and the roasted hen is immediately discovered hidden in the pantry. With a second conjuration James produces the drinks, to Hab's delight. James then says that he will drive out of the house an evil spirit in disguise as a priest, provided Hab will beat him over the head with a club as he leaves. The wife now realizes the worst, but is reassured by James in lines 235–40:

BESSY be this began to smell   *by*
A Rat, but kept her Mind to'r sell;
She pray'd like Howdy in her Drink,   *a midwife*
But mean time tipt young *James* a Wink.
James frae his Eye an Answer sent,
Which made the Wife right well content.

The terrified priest is beaten by Hab on his way out, and the
tale ends with an excellent punch-line from the mouth of the
gullible miller:

I trow, quoth he, *I laid well on;*
But wow he's like our ain Mess John!   *own Priest*

"The Monk and the Miller's Wife" is sketchy in characterization, but has a fine narrative movement to a hilarious climax.
It lacks the subtleties of style in the great fabliaux of Chaucer
or even in "The Freiris of Berwick"; Burns Martin is right in
observing that Ramsay is "unable to catch the fine flavour of
his model."[10] Nevertheless, the tale has merit as a piece of
brilliant narrative verse—boisterous, earthy, fast-moving, colloquial Scots, with the rhythms of living speech. Burns must have
learned much from it about the possibilities of Scots tetrameter
couplets for narrative purposes, possibilities that found their
fullest and richest expression in "Tam o' Shanter."[11] On the
whole, "The Monk and the Miller's Wife" is Ramsay's most
distinguished narrative poem; indeed, it is the finest extended
piece of Scots narrative verse of the eighteenth century before
Burns.

We come finally to "The Miller and his Man" (*STS*, 3:203–
9), a sequel to "The Monk and the Miller's Wife" that Ramsay,
unaccountably, chose not to publish. Based on a folk motif similar to that of Chaucer's *Reeve's Tale,* this lively fabliau is almost
as good as Ramsay's earlier effort. Its plot can be summarized
briefly. The miller, Haby, is married to Bessie, but lusts after
their maid, Jean. The two women get together and plan to
fool Haby by changing beds. Jean pretends to agree to a secret
rendezvous with the miller, and Haby spends the night in bed
with his wife, thinking he is with Jean. Worried about a possible
pregnancy and scandal, Hab encourages his servant Jock to try

his luck with Jean, which he does successfully—with Bessie. In the morning Bessie reveals the trick and the truth comes out. She is so appreciative that she serves her husband special eggs for breakfast (lines 199–208):

> quoth Bessie, smirkingly and leugh,[12]   *laughed*
> trowth ye deserve them well eneugh,   *enough*
> for I'm right certain since yestreen,   *last night*
> Ye've playd a manly part with Jean,
> as ye imagined, while kind she
> transfer'd your favors oer to me,
> sae that instead of a young Lassie
> you only kissd your ain auld Bessy,   *own old*
> and I'll refer'd now to your sell,
> If ye can ony difference tell.

"The Miller and his Man" is spirited stuff, with much the same kind of broad humor, galloping pace, and rich vernacular as in "The Monk and the Miller's Wife." Like its predecessor, it is a small masterpiece of folk wit.

Summary

Ramsay's narrative poetry in Scots extends over a considerable range, both in genres and in quality. His imitations of Middle Scots verse have been unduly belittled in recent times, and chiefly because of his necessarily superficial or inadequate knowledge of the older Scots tongue. Yet in the satiric allegory of "The Vision," at least, he achieved very creditable results. Several of his adaptations of the French fables of La Motte and La Fontaine, as we have seen, have genuine vigor and a folksy charm that are characteristically his own, not to be found in his sources. On the other hand, those fables invented by Ramsay himself tend to be pointless or insipid. Finally, in the comic tale or fabliau he produced two specimens, "The Monk and the Miller's Wife" and "The Miller and his Man," that are masterly in their genre and showed his successors the potential of modern Scots for this kind of comic poetry.

Chapter Seven

Ramsay in English Dress

It is startling to recall that close to half of Ramsay's total poetic output is not in Scots at all, but in standard literary English. The same is true, more or less, of the works of Fergusson and of Burns as well, and for the same reasons. The divided culture of Lowland Scotland in the eighteenth century made it inevitable that even such intensely patriotic native poets would attempt to write in both idioms. English was the more prestigious language with a major literature both in the past and in the present, from Chaucer, through Shakespeare, Spenser, and Milton, to Dryden and Pope—a literature known and admired throughout the civilized world. When Ramsay started, Scotland had not had an important literature for well over a century; its poetic glory was all in the medieval past. To be taken seriously as a Scottish poet, then, Ramsay felt that he must also write in fashionable English to show that he was something more than a provincial oddity, that he was a versatile man of letters and part of the mainstream of European culture. Though they spoke Scots in everyday usage, the Scottish gentry, professional people and literati, whom Ramsay had to interest in order to be accepted at all, themselves wrote in English or tried to, and they expected him to do the same, at least to some extent. Consequently, the pressures of English influence upon Ramsay were intense and well nigh irresistible.

As all critics have noted, Ramsay's poems in English are, as a rule, markedly inferior to those in his native tongue. And this difference, too, was inevitable. David Craig is surely correct in arguing that Ramsay (and Fergusson and Burns) could never be truly at home in literary English, could never be comfortable in that idiom in the way that his southern contemporaries like Gay or Pope could be, simply because he did not speak in it.[1] After all, Ramsay had been born and brought up in rural Lanarkshire and had learned there the colloquial Scots that was his natural language for the rest of his life, the language in which he could most readily think and feel. Standard English, and more particularly the stylized "poetic diction" that eighteenth-century genteel poets were expected to write in, was always slightly foreign and therefore difficult for him. With practice, of course, he acquired a moderate competence, but he could never find a way to give vent to his deepest feelings in literary English, or even to express any idea with complete naturalness and conviction. Let us turn now to look at a few examples of his English verse.

Early Poems in English

One of the earliest of Ramsay's longer poems is "The Morning Interview" (*STS*, 1:1–9), first published separately in 1716 and then given the place of honor as the first item in his handsome volume of *Poems* in 1721. Though Ramsay uses four lines from Waller as his motto, the poem is in fact based on Pope's *The Rape of the Lock,* and is a rather pale imitation of that brilliant social satire. He goes so far as to borrow, quite unabashedly, the idea of *"Sylphs"* (lines 69–70) from Pope, and even a lap-dog by the name of "Shock" (line 164) and the notion of a petticoat as a "ten-fold Fence" (line 147). Apart from incidental details of this kind, Ramsay labors mightly but unsuccessfully to catch something of the scintillating style of Pope's heroic couplets. A few lines will suffice to show this (85–92):

> To her Apartment straight the daring Swain
> Approach'd and softly knock'd, nor knock'd in vain.
> The Nymph new wak'd starts from the lazy Down,
> And rolls her gentle Limbs in Morning-Gown:
> But half-awake, she judges it must be
> *Frankalia* come to take her Morning Tea;
> Cries, Welcome, Cousin. But she soon began
> To change her Visage, when she saw a Man.

This is not Pope, of course, but perhaps Ramsay seems rather flat only in comparison to the dazzling sophistication of his master here. Actually, "The Morning Interview" is not bad when seen as a youthful, ambitious experiment in modish English

vers de société. Ramsay is straining for his effects, but the poem
is certainly competent and shows some talent.

Much less pleasing is "Tartana, or the Plaid" (*STS*, 1:27–
37), a patriotic poem in praise of home-bred Scottish clothing,
as opposed to newfangled foreign fashions. It was published
separately in 1718, and there were two more editions in 1719
and 1720. In the last of these Ramsay tried the unique experiment of "translating" his own English poem into Scots, but
even that could not redeem it aesthetically. When he included
it in his 1721 *Poems* Ramsay returned to the English version.
The problem with "Tartana" is the incredible stiffness and fatu-
ousness of its style. Take lines 25–29 for example:

> Be strong each Thought, run soft each happy Line,
> That Gracefulness and Harmony will shine,
> Adapted to the beautiful Design.
> Great is the Subject, vast th' exalted Theme,
> And shall stand fair in endless Rolls of Fame.

This is empty and insipid enough, but far worse is a couplet
farther on (lines 242–43) where Ramsay describes a Scottish
lady's breast in these terms:

> So through *Hamilla*'s op'ned Plaid, we may
> Behold her heavenly Face, and heaving Milky Way.

From time to time Ramsay is capable, as here, of the most
unbelievably poor taste, especially when he is laboring to be
impressive. It would be tedious to give many examples of "bad
Ramsay," but any reader may find them plentiful in "Tartana,"
a thoroughly bad poem that runs, or limps, to 368 lines.

Of Ramsay's other early pieces in English heroic couplets
only two or three deserve mention. "Edinburgh's Address to
the Country. November, 1718" (*STS*, 1:53–56) is ambitious
but generally uninspired. "Content. A Poem" (*STS*, 1:90–105),
first published in 1719, is Ramsay's longest poem in English
with 518 lines. It is an extended philosophical allegory, with
some themes and human types similar to those in Henry

Vaughan's celebrated poem, "The World." Ramsay's style is very uneven here: some passages are well and smoothly written, others are flat, strained, or overly inflated. Ramsay's characteristically high opinion of himself, an attitude that is sometimes irritating but that the poet no doubt intended to be taken facetiously, appears in an early section (lines 29–32) that will serve to illustrate the quality of the whole:

> HAIL blest Content! who art by Heav'n design'd
> Parent of Health and Chearfulness of Mind;
> Serene Content shall animate my Song,
> And make the immortal Numbers smooth and strong.

"Content" is a long, pretentious piece that fails to rise above the level of competence.

Slightly more interesting is a tribute to the Duke of Hamilton, published in 1720, and entitled "Clyde's Welcome to his Prince" (*STS,* 1:233–35). This, too, is in English neoclassical heroic couplets, but it is notable for a rather imaginative personification of the river Clyde and of its tributary, the little river Evan, which joins the Clyde near Hamilton, not far from Ramsay's native village of Leadhills. Stylistically, however, the poem is marred by inflated rhetoric.

English Poems of the 1720s

After the success of *Poems* (1721), Ramsay continued to compose in English with undiminished energy, while he was simultaneously producing far more valuable work in Scots. Between 1721 and 1728 he wrote four major poems in English, none of which is successful. "Health: A Poem" (*STS,* 2:5–17), first published separately in 1724, is a long, pedestrian piece on the prime importance of good health, the avoidance of vice and excess, the art of keeping well. It belongs to the curious neoclassical genre of the "arts" poem, the versified "how-to-do-it" of which an exceptional specimen is John Gay's *Trivia,* on the art of walking the streets of London. But whereas *Trivia* is enlivened with interesting detail and ironic wit, "Health" is a "straight" treatment of its subject, relatively uninspired. An

average passage may be seen in lines 249–54, the beginning
of Ramsay's attack upon the excesses of winebibbing:

> WHOEVER's tempted to transgress the Line,
> By Moderation fix'd to enlivening Wine;
> View *Macro* wasted long before his time,
> Whose Head, bow'd down, proclaims his liquid Crime.
> The Purple Dye, with Ruby Pimples mixt,
> As witnesses upon his Face are fixt.

The feeling of strain comes out in phrases like "his liquid
Crime." This is competent but labored versification, and it goes
on for 423 lines.

A comparable work, also in heroic couplets, is "The General
Mistake: A Satyre" (*STS,* 2:118–24), which is a series of character portraits of various types of fools. It obviously owes much
in a general way to passages in the works of the great English
satirists, especially Dryden's *Absalom and Achitophel* and *MacFlecknoe* and Pope's *The Dunciad.* But Ramsay's wit here is thin
and forced, sometimes so much so as to be almost unintelligible.
"The Nuptials, A Masque on the Marriage of his Grace James
Duke of Hamilton and Brandon, &c." (*STS,* 2:94–103), first
published separately in 1723, is a more pretentious effort and
even less successful. After his first fame as a poet Ramsay was
often tempted to flatter his influential acquaintances with occasional pieces of this kind, usually with disastrous results artistically. "The Nuptials" is one of the worst of his major poems,
very pompous and stilted, not worth quoting.

A fourth extensive work of this period in prettified English,
with the faintest tincture of Scots, is "The Fair Assembly: A
Poem" (*STS,* 2:129–35). This is composed in the "Christis
Kirk" stanza without the tag-line, and is a genteel piece in praise
of and in defense of Edinburgh's "Assembly," where the gentry
regularly gathered for dancing. Ramsay addresses specifically
the *"Caledonian* Nymphs" who attended these affairs, and he
emphasizes the idea that dancing is a healthful and invigorating
exercise. In the midst of the most polite verses, however, the
poem is marred by a surprisingly sensual passage describing
Bellinda's "Breasts like driven Snaw" (lines 73–76):

> Like Lilly-banks see how they rise,
>   With a fair Glen between,
> Where living Streams, blew as the Skies,
>   Are branching upward seen.

Since Ramsay's aim was to defend the Assembly against the censure of the rigid puritans of Edinburgh, stressing its chasteness and sobriety, these lines seem not only in rather bad taste, but incredibly ill advised. As Daiches says in another connection, "We never know what Ramsay is going to do."[2] In other respects "The Fair Assembly" is a competent piece of work.

Songs in English

During the early and middle phases of his career, when Ramsay was producing some major poems and dozens of shorter ones in neoclassical English, he was also producing songs in the same fashionable mode, though usually set to Scottish tunes. His motive seems to have been patriotic and worthy enough: he aimed to preserve the old Scots melodies by providing them with polite and cultivated words that would make them suitable for singing by Scottish ladies and gentlemen in the drawing rooms and salons of Edinburgh. The artistic results, unfortunately, were generally abysmal. All of Ramsay's English songs are poetically weak and artificial, some worse than others.

Among his early songs in English the most notorious failure is "The Kind Reception" (*STS*, 1:45–46), Ramsay's words for the great Scots tune of "Auld Lang Syne," later immortalized by Burns. It opens as follows:

> Should auld Acquaintance be forgot,
>   Tho they return with Scars?
> These are the noble Heroe's Lot,
>   Obtain'd in glorious Wars.

And so forth—further quotation would be painful. Ramsay composed literally dozens of songs like this, infinitely duller than those for which he wrote Scots lyrics, as we have seen in an earlier chapter, and they need not delay us here.

One other of Ramsay's later English songs, however, has a special interest in relation to Burns. It is entitled "To L. M. M." (*STS,* 3:43), and is set to the lively Scottish tune of "Rantin roaring Willie." Ramsay printed it as his own in *The Tea-Table Miscellany,* and it is probably addressed to Lady Mary Montgomery.[3] This undistinguished lyric appears to have supplied Burns with important images for his very fine song of "Mary Morison."[4] Here is the first half of Ramsay's opening stanza and the whole of his third:

> O MARY! thy graces and glances,
>   Thy smiles so inchantingly gay,
> And thoughts so divinely harmonious,
>   Clear wit and good humour display.

> Thus looks the poor beggar on treasure,
>   And shipwreck'd on landskips on shore,
> Be still more divine, and have pity;
>   I die soon as hope is no more.
> For, MARY, my soul is thy captive,
>   Nor loves, nor expects, to be free;
> Thy beauties are fetters delightful,
>   Thy slavery's a pleasure to me.

Compare with this insipid stuff the first six lines of "Mary Morison":

> O Mary, at thy window be,
>   It is the wish'd, the trysted hour;   *appointed*
> Those smiles and glances let me see,
>   That makes the miser's treasure poor:
> How blythely wad I bide the stoure,   *adversity*
>   A weary slave frae sun to sun. . . .

There are further echoes of Ramsay in Burns's final stanza, but what is given above is surely enough to show the relationship between the two songs. Burns's "O Mary" followed by "smiles and glances" parallels Ramsay's opening, just as his "miser's treasure poor" follows Ramsay's "poor beggar on treasure," and his "weary slave" image echoes Ramsay's final two lines. What happened here in all probability, is that Burns read Ram-

say's pallid song carefully in *The Tea-Table Miscellany;* a cluster
of its images stuck in his subconscious memory and emerged
later in "Mary Morison," metamorphosed by the alchemy of
art into a beautiful lyric. It is an extraordinary example of a
first-rate poem inspired by a third-rate one.

Later Poems in English

Through the long final phase of Ramsay's career from 1728
to 1758 he continued to write poems in English as well as
Scots, but almost exclusively for private circulation. The bulk
of these are occasional pieces such as the amusing squib he
inserted in a letter to his good friend Sir John Clerk, concerning
one of the minor pleasures of old age (*STS*, 4:227):

> of all delights that gain regard
> of which the Mob of Mortalls Crack O'   *talk of*
> thers none on Earth to be Compar'd
> to sit & shite & smoak tabaco

This is immediately followed up by some charming advice to
Clerk in prose: "Farwell, be chearfull, live contented and tem-
perately, keep a clear conscience and be afraid of nothing. Re-
joyce in the wife of your youth & and be delighted [?] with
your offspring, so shall your Days flow Easy, and nights be
refreshful and when old age comes you will know as little about
[it] as I do."

Most of Ramsay's later English verse is unpublished trivia
of this kind, but there are a few exceptions. The best of these
is "An Elegy in Memory of William Aikman" (*STS*, 3:217–
20). Aikman was a close friend of Ramsay's, a Scottish painter
of some distinction who moved to London in 1723 and died
there in 1731.[5] Ramsay's poem is a fairly moving tribute,
smoothly written in standard literary English in tetrameter quatrains (*a b a b*). Here is one of the better stanzas (lines 37–
40):

> How vain the Medling Mind of Man
> that with his Narrow Bounded Sence
> attempts complaint, or dares to Scan
> the Maze divine of Providence

These are conventional pieties, it is true, but they are surprisingly well expressed. The elegy proves that Ramsay, when he was not trying to be impressive, could do well enough in the English idiom. No doubt the distinction of this poem results at least partly from the fact that here Ramsay was giving vent to real feelings about his old friend—and not for publication. Why did he leave unpublished a poem as expert and genuine as this? We can only guess that he may have felt that it was *too* personal. At any rate, the elegy on Aikman is one of Ramsay's very few pieces in English that come anywhere close to poetic success.

Summary

As a poet Ramsay was never comfortable in neoclassical English, yet he persisted. The pressures on him to do so, as we have seen, were very strong, especially after the success of *Poems* (1721). No doubt his aristocratic and literary friends in Edinburgh, who were addicted to this kind of inflated, sentimental poetry, advised him to continue. Burns, sixty years later, was to hear exactly the same kind of wrongheaded advice: Scots was too limiting; in English he could command a far wider audience; also, English was more "dignified." But for the writing of poetry, which depends so much upon subtle nuances of language, English was fundamentally unnatural to Ramsay, as to Burns. Hence his overall failure in the southern "poetic" idiom. In everything from pretentious philosophical poems to brief songs he rarely attained an English style that rose above dullness and insipidity.

Chapter Eight

Ramsay as Anthologist and Publicist of Scottish Poetry

Quite apart from his original poetic work, Ramsay expended a large part of his considerable energies as a publisher and editor of Scottish poetry, as an antiquarian, and as a propagandist for the Scots poetic revival of the eighteenth century. At the very beginning of his literary career he became involved in the collection of Scottish songs and of specimens of Middle Scots poetry, activities that eventually culminated in his two epoch-making anthologies, *The Tea-Table Miscellany* and *The Ever Green.*

Preliminaries

Precisely when Ramsay began collecting tunes and texts of Scots folk songs is uncertain, but it was probably as early as his Easy Club days, about 1715 or so. The first concrete evidence of his interest in this field was the publication in 1718 of a pamphlet entitled *Scots Songs,* by "A. Ramsay," consisting of seven songs, to which three more were added in the second edition of 1719, and another three in 1720; all thirteen were then reprinted in *Poems* (1721). Still another set of eight *Scots Songs* appeared in pamphlet form in 1720, probably by popular demand, and they too found their way into Ramsay's collected edition of 1721.[1] Of these twenty-one early songs, only seven are in Scots—"Bessy Bell and Mary Gray," "The Young Laird and Edinburgh Katy," "Katy's Answer," "O'er Bogie," "I'll never leave thee," "Polwart on the Green," and "Up in the Air." The bulk of them are efforts by Ramsay to compose prettified English words for traditional Scottish melodies. Through all of these years prior to 1723 Ramsay must have been gradually gathering and studying the Scots tunes that formed the basis of his work. Altogether, his early attempts met with immediate popular success and served as preparatory work for his ambitious anthology. Encouraged by a rising tide of public acceptance of his Scots songs, Ramsay was ready in 1723 to launch *The Tea-Table Miscellany*. During these same years Ramsay became deeply engrossed in the study and preservation of the remains of Middle Scots poetry. As we have seen, as early as 1715 he was busy in this field, composing canto 2 of "Christis Kirk on the Green" in that year, adding canto 3 in 1718, and from 1718 onward publishing edition after edition of the old poem together with his own sequels. For these separate editions of the fifteenth-century "Christis Kirk" in pamphlet form, Ramsay adopted substantially the text as he found it in James Watson's *Choice Collection* of 1706. But in 1718 he made a crucial discovery. He learned of the existence of the vast and priceless Bannatyne Manuscript of 1568 which he was able to borrow from its owner, William Carmichael of Skirling, a wealthy and eminent Scottish lawyer and brother of the Earl of Hyndford.[2] This must have been a thrilling "find" for Ramsay, who promptly threw himself into the study of the rich medieval poetry of Scotland as he found it in Bannatyne, even to the extent of composing a few imitations of Middle Scots of his own invention. His enthusiasm for the older native poetry, and his patriotic urge to preserve this treasure and to publicize it, culminated six years later in the publication in two volumes of *The Ever Green* (1724), Ramsay's extraordinary anthology of Middle Scots poems culled largely from the Bannatyne Manuscript.

The Tea-Table Miscellany

Ramsay issued the first volume of his Scots song anthology in 1723. So phenomenal was its success that he steadily expanded the project over the ensuing years. A second volume was published in 1726, a third in 1727, and a fourth in 1737. During Ramsay's lifetime at least fourteen editions of *The Tea-Table Miscellany* appeared, in various combinations of one, three, or four volumes, not counting large selections that were reprinted in other anthologies such as *Orpheus Caledonius* and *The Charmer* published in London.[3] Altogether, it was the most hugely popular and lucrative of all Ramsay's ventures as editor and publisher.

It is clear now that Ramsay, in compiling *The Tea-Table Miscellany,* had several quite different purposes—some were patriotic and wholly admirable, others were expedient or commercial. Certainly, he aimed at preserving the older Scottish melodies (some of which might have been lost otherwise), not so much by printing the musical notation, but by providing singable words that he hoped would help to perpetuate the tunes. That such was his most important motive is suggested by the fact that he stressed the beauty of the tunes in the opening sentences of his "Preface" to the *Miscellany* (*STS*, 4:238–40): "Altho' it be acknowledged, that our *Scots* Tunes have not lengthened Variety of Musick, yet they have an agreeable Gaiety and natural Sweetness, that makes them acceptable wherever they are known, not only among our selves, but in other Countries. They are for the most part so chearful, that on hearing them well play'd or sung, we find a Difficulty to keep our selves from dancing." Ramsay's interest in Scots *music* as such is further evidenced by his publication in 1725 of a volume of *Musick for Allan Ramsay's Collection of Scots Songs,* prepared by an obscure Edinburgh musician, Alexander Stuart, with Ramsay's assistance, as a companion piece to the first volume of the *Miscellany.* There can be no doubt about his desire to save traditional Scottish melodies from oblivion.

Another of Ramsay's aims in this anthology, though a much less urgent one, was to record and publicize some of the old words for Scots tunes, before they, too, were forgotten. To this end he printed a few of the traditional lyrics (provided they were relatively inoffensive), but in this effort he was far less assiduous than his successors later in the century, such as David Herd, Robert Burns, or Sir Walter Scott. No doubt Ramsay's attempt to recover old words was rather feeble because it was in conflict with his third purpose in *The Tea-Table Miscellany,* to make the old tunes respectable in the highest social circles by providing "polite" lyrics for them. Many of the old words were too rough for the fashionable parlors of Edinburgh and London, especially for the high-born ladies whom Ramsay especially wanted to have on his side. In his "Preface" he says as much: "In my Compositions and Collections, I have kept out all Smut and Ribaldry, that the modest Voice and Ear of the fair Singer might meet with no Affront; the chief Bent of all my Studies being, to gain their good Graces: And it shall always be my Care, to ward off these Frowns that would prove mortal to my Muse." It is easy to smile at this mildly facetious manifesto, but behind it lay a hard economic fact. Ramsay was exploiting an already established fondness for Scots songs in modish Edinburgh and (he hoped) London, but he knew only too well that in order to sell his expensive anthology he would have to make it fully acceptable to the kind of people (especially the ladies) who could afford to buy it. Hence his shrewd and deliberate strategy of "politeness." Without such an editorial policy, the *Miscellany* would probably have got nowhere; Ramsay was by no means a prude himself, but by making this kind of compromise he made possible the fulfillment of his other and larger purposes.

A fourth aim underlying *The Tea-Table Miscellany* was to make available a means of formal publication for composers of new lyrics for older tunes, including himself and the group of younger poets whom he took under his wing. As he states, again, in his "Preface," over sixty of the lyrics in the first two volumes were of his own composition, but "About thirty more were done by some ingenious young Gentlemen, who were so pleased with my Undertaking, that they generously lent me their Assistance." Foremost among these "ingenious young Gentlemen" were Robert Crawford, William Hamilton of Bangour, David Mallet, and Hamilton of Gilbertfield, but there were others (mostly unidentified) as well.[4] Thus Ramsay provided encouragement for the idea that *new* words could be written for the old Scots tunes, an idea that led ultimately to the consummate lyrics of Burns. In *The Tea-Table Miscellany* Ramsay's purposes were certainly mixed, but on the whole they were worthy.

The contents of Ramsay's anthology were shrewdly calculated to fulfill these multiple aims. The tunes themselves are overwhelmingly Scottish, though not exclusively so; but the lyrics are a different story. The words for the roughly four hundred songs in *The Tea-Table Miscellany* fall into five categories, as follows: (1) Some of them are genuine old Scottish folk songs and ballads, often doctored by Ramsay to make them wholly acceptable to his fastidious audience. (2) Several consist of old Scots words "with additions" by Ramsay himself. (3) A third group is made up of popular English songs, mostly by unknown authors. (4) A large number are new words by Ramsay, in Scots or in English. (5) Finally, there are many new lyrics, mostly in English, by his "ingenious young Gentlemen" collaborators. In his introductory material, Ramsay provided a sort of code to indicate his sources, announcing that songs "marked C, D, H, L, M, O, &c. are new words by different hands; X, the authors unknown; Z, old songs; Q, old songs with additions"— but this was a very halfhearted effort, since fewer than a third of the songs in the first two volumes are actually coded this way, and in the last two volumes there are no attributions at all. Over eighty of the items in the anthology are by Ramsay himself, as he tells us and as we know from other evidence, yet only two of these are marked with an "R," so that his coding system is haphazard in the extreme and is virtually useless. Let us turn now to the individual volumes, where some interesting patterns are observable.

Volume 1 contains one hundred songs, of which precisely one half are more or less in Scots, the other half in English. Of the fifty Scots songs, twelve are coded with "Z" or "Q" (old, or old with additions), and these include such traditional folk songs as "Muirland Willie," "Auld Rob Morris," "The Blythsome Bridal," and "The auld Wife beyont the Fire." A few others, such as Ramsay's own refurbishment of "O'er Bogie," should probably have been marked with a "Q." The grand old song of "The Gaberlunzieman," often attributed to King James V of Scotland, is mysteriously coded "I" (possibly for "James"). A very few modern Scots songs apart from those by the editor are there also, including two apparently attributed to William Hamilton of Gilbertfield (they are marked "W" and "W. W.," from Hamilton's nickname of "Wanton Willie"). Fully half of the first volume, however, consists of rather stilted English lyrics in the genteel style, with five attributed to Robert Crawford and many by Ramsay himself.

In volume 2 the proportion of Scots to English lyrics is about the same—that is, half and half. Here again we have a dozen or so specimens of lively older songs such as "Todlen butt, and todlen ben," "Rob's Jock came to woo our Jenny," and "Waly, waly, gin love be bonny," as well as a pallid reworking

of the ballad of "William and Margaret" attributed to "D. M."
(David Mallet). The very last item in the volume is William
Hamilton of Bangour's beautiful modern version of "The Braes
of Yarrow." There are other notable pieces, but, again, half
of the volume is in dull, sentimental English. Volume 3 goes
all the way in that direction, with no Scots lyrics at all. Quite
possibly Ramsay, encouraged by the enthusiasm of his aristocratic patrons for the more genteel songs rather than the colloquial native ones in his first two volumes, decided to cater
exclusively to the fashionable taste this time. Volume 3 consists
mainly of popular *English* songs, prettified with "poetic" diction.
He even includes, without credit, the celebrated seventeenth-
century lyric of Sir John Suckling, "Why so pale and wan, fond
lover?" Apart from such brilliant exceptions, the songs in this
volume are generally undistinguished sets of modish clichés.

In his fourth and final volume Ramsay returned to a mixture
of Scots and English lyrics, though with a heavy bias in favor
of the latter idiom. There are twenty-one English songs from
John Gay's *Beggar's Opera,* but Ramsay also prints at least thirteen
Scots songs, including a handful of the great old folk ballads
such as "Bonny Barbara Allan" and "Rare Willy drown'd in
Yarrow." In this last installment of his massive anthology Ramsay no doubt felt secure enough in its financial success to go
back to his patriotic motive of preserving something of the old
Scots words as well as the traditional tunes.

Despite its obvious weaknesses from scholarly or aesthetic
points of view, *The Tea-Table Miscellany* is an extraordinary accomplishment. It is the pioneer anthology of Scots song, the
first of a long series of such books that culminated at the end
of the century in the monumental collections of James Johnson
(*The Scots Musical Museum*) and George Thomson (*A Select Collection of Original Scotish Airs for the Voice*), in which Burns was
to play a vital role.[5] As Kinghorn says (*STS,* 4:147), until the
publication of David Herd's scholarly anthology of 1776 Ramsay's *Miscellany* held a place of honor as "the most 'Scottish'
of all eighteenth-century collections." Ramsay's ambitious work
was the first, and it remained (in most respects) the best of its
kind for half a century. Its very big success and wide circulation
were crucially important in establishing Scots song on a permanent basis as a vibrant part of the cultural life of Scotland.

The Ever Green

Subsequent to his exciting discovery of the Bannatyne Manuscript in 1718, Ramsay's study of medieval Scottish poetry resulted in the publication in 1724 of *The Ever Green*. Some years earlier James Watson had included a few specimens of the older poetry in his *Choice Collection* (1706, 1709, 1711), but Ramsay's was the first anthology ever published to be devoted exclusively to the works of the Middle Scots makars. His nationalistic aims are made clear in a rather eloquent "Preface" (*STS*, 4:236–38). "There is nothing," he says, "can be heard more silly than one's expressing his *Ignorance* of his *native Language*." His opposition to foreign affectations is more fully detailed in the following paragraphs:

When these good old *Bards* wrote, we had not yet made Use of imported Trimming upon our Cloaths, nor of Foreign Embroidery in our Writings. Their *Poetry* is the Product of their own Country, not pilfered and spoiled in the Transportation from abroad: Their Images are native, and their Landskips domestic; copied from those Fields and Meadows we every Day behold.

The *Morning* rises (in the Poets Description) as she does in the Scottish Horizon. We are not carried to *Greece* or *Italy* for a Shade, a stream or a Breeze. The *Groves* rise in our own Valleys; the *Rivers* flow from our own Fountains, and the *Winds* blow upon our own Hills. I find not Fault with those Things, as they are in *Greece* or *Italy*: But with a *Northern Poet* for fetching his Materials from these Places, in a Poem, of which his own Country is the Scene; as our *Hymners* to the *Spring* and *Makers* of *Pastorals* frequently do.

Ramsay is expressing here not only his patriotic admiration of the Middle Scots makars, but also a vindication of his own practice in using the Scots language and in domesticating the pastoral tradition in *The Gentle Shepherd* and elsewhere. He wished to rescue the old poets from undeserved neglect and, at the same time, to represent himself as a worthy successor in a proud national tradition.

Generally speaking, Ramsay's motives in *The Ever Green* were more admirable and less commercial than in *The Tea-Table Miscellany*. His hopes for the anthology, however, were ambitious. Toward the end of his preface he plainly states his intention to publish a third and fourth volume of *The Ever Green,* including further large selections from the Bannatyne Manuscript, plus his own biographical sketches of the medieval Scots poets. Unfortunately, these designs never materialized, for the simple reason that the first two volumes fell far short of the popular success of Ramsay's song anthology. In *The Ever Green* he was attempting to stimulate or revive an antiquarian literary interest, whereas in the *Miscellany* he was exploiting a popular fondness for Scots song that was already well established. Hence the latter turned out to be a spectacular commercial success, while *The Ever Green* did not sell very well and the two volumes saw only one edition in Ramsay's lifetime. After all, the old poems required considerable effort to understand and appreciate; they appealed, by their very nature, to a reading public of studious literary tastes—a decidedly limited market in his time or in any time. Nevertheless, of his two anthologies Ramsay's *Ever Green* is much the greater achievement.

Ramsay's editorial methods in *The Ever Green* were, inevitably, amateurish. In his day there were no scholars in the field of Middle Scots; as a serious editor of this poetry Ramsay himself was, in fact, the pioneer. Later in the century he came under severe criticism for his methods by more learned editors such as Lord Hailes and John Pinkerton. Hailes exaggerated Ramsay's editorial lapses, and the snobbish Pinkerton attacked him in grossly unfair terms, calling him "a buffoon" with "no spark of genius," and sneering at him as "one of the mob, both in education and in mind."[6] Pinkerton's incredibly nasty remarks, which have disgraced him far more than Ramsay, were no doubt motivated by his resentment of Ramsay's broad popularity.

Still, these early strictures, though partly discounted in recent times, have influenced twentieth-century views of Ramsay as editor. Much too much has been made, for example, of Ramsay's notorious "Postscript" to William Dunbar's great poem, "Lament for the Makaris," as printed in *The Ever Green.* To this impressive work with its sonorous Latin refrain, *Timor mortis conturbat me* ("the fear of death troubles me"), Ramsay added three stanzas of his own (*STS,* 3:97):

SUTHE I forsie, if Spae-craft   *in truth; foresee; prophecy*
    had,   *hold*

Frae Hethir-Muirs sall ryse   *shall rise*
    a LAD,
Aftir twa Centries pas, sall he   *centuries pass*
    Revive our Fame and
    Memorie.

Then sall we flourish EVIR
    GRENE;
All thanks to carefull *Bannantyne,*
And to the PATRON kind
    and frie,   *generous*
    Quha lends the LAD baith   *who*
    them and me.

FAR sall we fare, baith Eist
    and West,
Owre ilka Clyme by *Scots*   *over every clime*
    possest;
Then sen our Warks sall nevir die,   *since; works*
    Timor mortis non   (*fear of death does not*
    turbat me.   *trouble me*)
                    Quod DUNBAR.

Some modern critics have been horrified by this piece of impudence, seeing it as an inexcusable desecration of a great poem.[7] But Ramsay was not trying to deceive his readers into thinking that the third-rate stanzas of the postscript were actually by Dunbar; he attached a footnote identifying "PATRON" as William Carmichael "who lent A. R. that curious MSS. collected by Mr. *George Bannantyne, Anno* 1568, from whence these Poems are printed"—thus making it entirely clear that the stanzas were added by himself. Hence, the "Postscript" is by no means an unscrupulous deception, but rather a kind of literary joke (admittedly an outrageous one) that Ramsay did not expect to be taken too seriously. At the same time, Kinghorn suggests (*STS,* 4:137), it was a means of "identifying himself with the spirit that had fired the medieval line of poets," poets whom Ramsay genuinely revered.

The modern scholarly attitude about the sanctity of literary texts was unknown in Ramsay's era, and it is no wonder that he did not share it. In *The Ever Green* he felt free to revise

lines that he thought were metrically deficient, or to paraphrase
whole passages that he did not fully understand or would prove
baffling to his readers. Above all, his aim was to provide a
readable text that would make the old poets as accessible as
possible to moderns, and this Ramsay succeeded in doing remarkably well. Kinghorn, in his excellent discussion of the anthology (*STS*, 4:128–41), amply documents the various kinds
of editorial "sins" that Ramsay committed from the twentieth-
century point of view, but he gives him full credit for admirable
motives and for what is, on the whole and despite lapses caused
by ignorance, a quite extraordinary accomplishment. Given the
rather dim lights that Ramsay was working by, *The Ever Green*
is a pioneer anthology of high merit.

Its contents, too, are generally praiseworthy. Apart from the
selections from Bannatyne, which make up three quarters of
the work, Ramsay included his own three imitations of older
Scots—"The Eagle and Robin Red-breist," "Hardyknute" (by
Lady Wardlaw and Ramsay), and "The Vision"—a few genuine
old songs and ballads, such as "Johnie Armstrang," and Alexander Montgomerie's lengthy allegory of *The Cherrie and the Slae*
which he found, as he tells us, in two old prints of 1597 and
1615. All the rest comes from the Bannatyne Manuscript and
is well chosen. "Christis Kirk on the Green" is there, of course,
attributed (by Bannatyne) to King James I. There are also gener-
ous samplings of the work of Robert Henryson and Alexander
Scott. Of Henryson we have the delightful "Robene and Makyne," "The Garmont of Gud Ladeis," and two of the best
of the *Fables;* from Scott, "The Justing and Debait" and several
elegant lyrics. Most fully represented of all is William Dunbar,
with twenty-three poems, including "The Thistle and the Rose,"
"Lament for the Makaris," "The Dance of the Sevin Deidly
Synnis," "A Generall Satyre," and many other pieces well chosen to illustrate the remarkable range of Dunbar's genius. In
addition, there are many specimens of unknown or uncertain
authorship, such as the hilarious "Wife of Auchtermuchty." Altogether, *The Ever Green* gives a skillfully chosen cross-section
of Middle Scots poetry in all of its astonishing richness and
variety, which is precisely what Ramsay was aiming to do.
Thanks to Ramsay's untiring effort, these "old *Bards*" came
alive in the two volumes of his *Ever Green,* which remained

for nearly half a century the best (and only) comprehensive anthology of Middle Scots poetry.

Summary

During all of his professional life Ramsay worked to spur a revival of interest in Scottish poetry—both as a glorious inheritance from the nation's past and as a creative opportunity for the future—in the face of increasing pressures of English and other foreign influences. Against all odds, he succeeded. An important part of that campaign was, obviously, his relentless effort as publisher, anthologist, and propagandist for Scots poetry. From his earliest days in the publishing business about 1718 until his retirement from active affairs in 1740, Ramsay gave much of his energy to this patriotic cause.

The most significant results of his exertions in this area were his two impressive anthologies, *The Tea-Table Miscellany* and *The Ever Green*. In the former, as we have seen, he felt obliged for practical reasons to compromise with fashionable tastes. Yet, by providing new lyrics (with the help of several collaborators) he managed to preserve for posterity hundreds of the older Scots tunes, many of which might have otherwise died out. He also offered an outlet for new creative work and set a precedent that led directly to Burns, as well as recording in print the traditional words for a couple of dozen old Scots songs and ballads. *The Ever Green* fell immeasurably short of the great popular and commercial success of the *Miscellany,* but in some respects it was even more important in making available the exciting Scots poetry of the medieval past. Though it is true that Ramsay's foremost successors in the eighteenth century, Fergusson and Burns, were seldom directly influenced by the work of the old makars, Ramsay's *Ever Green* gave them a taste of that vibrant, sophisticated native poetry and a crucial inkling of what could yet be done in the mother tongue. As a publicist for Scottish culture, "honest Allan" served his country very well.

Chapter Nine

Conclusion: Ramsay and the Future

It seems desirable at this point, before coming to an overall assessment of Allan Ramsay, to dispose of a general fallacy that has crept into Ramsay criticism over the years and has blurred the real nature of his achievement.

Perhaps the most serious mistake about Ramsay is the idea that his work as editor and publisher was as important as his creative endeavors as an original poet—or even more important historically. Thomas F. Henderson, writing in 1898, seems to have been the first to put forward this distorted view. After an unenthusiastic review of Ramsay's poetry, Henderson states flatly that "it is rather as editor than author that he occupies his peculiar place in the vernacular revival."[1] More recent critics have followed Henderson's lead, including David Daiches ("More important in some respects than Ramsay's original work was his work as an editor") and Alexander Kinghorn ("Ramsay is important as an antiquary no less than as an original poet")[2] This idea is surely mistaken, from any point of view. Ramsay's decisive impact in his own lifetime and afterward came from the *example* that he provided in his own poetry. Valuable as his function as anthologist was in making texts available, had Ramsay done nothing else he would be remembered today only as an obscure footnote to cultural history. The editing and publishing of Scots poetry would have proceeded with or without Ramsay. His own creative work in Scots was immeasurably more important and fruitful, because in it he demonstrated that the native tradition was still alive and feasible as a vehicle for new, modern poetic achievement. His successors—Fergusson, Burns, and others—admired and followed him not as an editor, but as a *Scots poet.* That was Ramsay's most vital contribution.

The Historic Importance of Ramsay's Work

Ramsay's influence upon later Scottish literature can be subsumed under several headings. He bequeathed to his successors a variety of important precedents in terms of verse forms, genres, and subject matters, as well as in his use of language and in his specific impact upon the work of his most distinguished followers in the eighteenth century—Robert Fergusson and Robert Burns.

From the very beginning of his career Ramsay revived and popularized four traditional Scottish meters: the "Christis Kirk" stanza, the *Cherrie and the Slae* stanza, the "Habbie" stanza, and the tetrameter couplet. By adopting the simplified form of the "Christis Kirk" meter, with a single dimeter tag-line ending in "that day" (which he found in Watson's *Choice Collection*), Ramsay established that version of the stanza as the standard for the eighteenth century and beyond, and he demonstrated its continuing vitality for modern purposes. Similarly, he revived the complex fourteen-line stanza of Alexander Montgomerie's *The Cherrie and the Slae* and passed it on to Burns. Most important of all was Ramsay's extensive use of the verse form of Sempill's "Habbie Simson," which Hamilton of Gilbertfield had tried out in "Bonnie Heck" a few years before Ramsay took it up. His skillful and versatile work in the "Habbie" form made it the most popular of all distinctively Scottish stanzas, and the favorite of both Fergusson and Burns. Finally, for narrative purposes in his fables and tales as well as in "A Tale of Three Bonnets" and other poems, Ramsay breathed new life into the tetrameter couplet, another medieval Scots verse form. By writing successfully in all of these traditional Scots meters, Ramsay revived their popularity and proved their feasibility for modern poetic purposes.

In the area of genres Ramsay's work was even more significant. He gave a vital new impetus to the old "Christis Kirk" tradition by writing lengthy sequels to the fifteenth-century poem. Taking his cue from Robert Sempill, he expanded the comic elegy form with several innovations, making it, too, an important Scots genre for the future. Similarly, he revitalized the type of the mock testament or "last dying words" poem. With the help of Hamilton of Gilbertfield he virtually created a wholly new genre in the Scots verse epistle, a distinctive form that was to be exploited brilliantly by Burns. Beyond that, Ramsay attempted with some success to elevate vernacular Scots poetry in dignity by composing free adaptations of some of the odes of Horace and by introducing serious pastoral elegies in the native tongue. From pastoral elegies he moved on to love eclogues in the same convention, and finally to his remarkable, full-length pastoral play of *The Gentle Shepherd.* At the same time Ramsay was the indispensable pioneer in the genre of Scots song, where his work both as editor and poet—but especially as an original lyricist—was to have immense results for the future, as we have seen. Furthermore, in his Scots fables and tales Ramsay achieved creditable results and showed the vigor and flexibility of Scots tetrameter couplets for narrative verse. In all of these genres Ramsay took initiatives of great historic importance.

In terms of subject matter Ramsay was equally versatile. He was brought up in a remote rural area, but lived all of his adult life in the small city of Edinburgh, so that he knew both worlds intimately; and this fact is reflected in the range of his poetry. In his continuations of "Christis Kirk," in parts of "A Tale of Three Bonnets," in many of his Scots songs and shorter pastorals, and, above all, in *The Gentle Shepherd,* Ramsay made effective use of his familiarity with the country life of Scotland in ways that were to affect the work of his successors, including Fergusson and, most obviously, Burns. Above all, however, Ramsay was the poet of Edinburgh—of the streets, clubs, and taverns of the crowded, squalid, beautiful old city that he loved. In his town satires Ramsay brought "Auld Reekie" vividly to life, and laid an essential foundation for the more brilliant satiric sketches of Robert Fergusson later in the century. As in so many areas of his work, Ramsay in his Edinburgh poems was the first modern Scots poet to show what could be done.

Ramsay's choice of Scots as the language of his most important poetry was crucial and, in a sense, revolutionary. Too much has been made by some commentators of the supposed degeneracy of the tongue that Ramsay inherited. Kinghorn, for example, speaks of "the poverty of Scots" and says that Ramsay "recognized that the language was not an adequate vehicle for expressing sophisticated ideas" (*STS,* 4:99–100). Yet Kinghorn and

Law, in an interesting headnote to their own glossary (*STS*, 6:200–201), estimate Ramsay's vocabulary of distinctively Scottish words at about 1,500, that of Burns at 2,500. When we consider the large vocabulary that is shared in common by Scots and English, this is hardly evidence of linguistic impoverishment. The recently completed *Scottish National Dictionary* (in ten volumes) is convincing proof of the astonishing richness of the Scots vocabulary for any kind of expression. Even in our era, when the cultural status of Scots is lower than in Ramsay's time, Hugh MacDiarmid was able to write in his native tongue *A Drunk Man Looks at the Thistle*, one of the masterpieces of sophisticated twentieth-century poetry. Ramsay's problem was not the impoverishment of the language itself, but rather the social *attitude* toward it and the lack of a continuous literary tradition. He was attempting to revive a poetic language that had been moribund for a century and a half, and was swimming against a strong current of anglicization among the Scottish gentry and professional classes. No individual writer, not even a man of transcendent genius like Burns, can change the course of cultural and linguistic history by his own unaided efforts, and it is no wonder that Ramsay did not succeed in reestablishing Scots as a literary language for all purposes. The wonder is that he did so well. By taking advantage of a surge of nationalistic emotion following the Union of 1707, by making various compromises, as we have seen, in language, style, and spelling, Ramsay managed to bring about a partial revival of Scottish poetry in the eighteenth century. He struggled valiantly to raise the cultural status of Scots by writing some serious poems in it, as well as the kind of jocular verse to which his readers were already accustomed. Without the foundations that he laid, without the broad audience that he gathered for Scots poetry, the later, more brilliant, work of Fergusson and Burns would scarcely have been possible.

The specific impact of Ramsay's work upon that of his successors has been indicated in previous chapters in treatments of individual poems, and it need only be summarized briefly here. His influence upon Robert Fergusson was, on the whole, a generalized one, in terms of genres, methods, and subject matters, rather than phraseology. Fergusson owes little to Ramsay stylistically, but a great deal in other respects. Among other things

Ramsay opened Fergusson's eyes to the potentialities of nearly all of the Scots genres in which he worked—the "Christis Kirk" tradition, verse epistle, Horatian ode, comic elegy, pastoral eclogue, Scots song—Fergusson followed him in all of these forms, in all of Ramsay's genres except the drama, and in all of Ramsay's verse forms except *The Cherrie and the Slae* stanza. In Ramsay's lively social satires of city life Fergusson found the precedent for the most important part of his life work; in poems like "A Tale of Three Bonnets" and "The Vision" he saw the opportunities for political satire in Scots; in *The Gentle Shepherd* and other pastorals the model for his own slightly idealized portraits of rural life in Scotland. It was no accident that when Fergusson first appeared on the literary scene in 1772 he was immediately hailed as a second Ramsay ("Is Allan risen frae the deid?").[3]

Ramsay's effect upon Burns, as we have seen in detail, was even more pervasive. We know that Burns read his Ramsay at a very early age, long before he discovered Fergusson; and he must have read all of Ramsay's poetry with deep concentration and delight, for it made a lasting impression on him. Not only did Burns, like Fergusson, try his hand at all of Ramsay's Scots genres (again with the exception of drama) and at all of his verse forms, but he was also affected in important ways by certain of Ramsay's techniques. Ramsay's use of ironic burlesque in "Elegy on John Cowper," for example, gave Burns a hint that he exploited with brilliant success in several of his greatest kirk satires. Similarly, many of Ramsay's specific themes, such as his mockery of rustic superstition and of religious hypocrisy, his contempt for foreign affectations in food, dress, and music, his strenuous championing of Scottish culture, and so forth, crop up over and over again in the writings of Burns. Beyond that, dozens of parallels of Ramsay's actual phrasing are to be found in Burns, including sometimes echoes of very inferior poems—showing that Burns knew *all* of Ramsay's work, good, bad, and indifferent. Stylistically, the impact of Fergusson on Burns was more electrifying than that of Ramsay, and that accounts for Burns's admiring comment on "the excellent Ramsay, and the still more excellent Ferguson [*sic*]."[4] Nevertheless, Ramsay's effect on Burns was multifaceted, extremely important, and generally salutary.

Altogether, Ramsay's importance in the history of Scots poetry is far-reaching. Almost single-handedly, through his indefatigable efforts both as poet and publicist, he managed to restore a decisive degree of respect for Scots poetry and for Scots language. He created or popularized nearly all of the important Scottish genres of the eighteenth-century revival, to such an extent that in the eyes of his countrymen in his own generation and until the advent of Burns he seemed to embody the entire movement—Ramsay himself *was* the Scots revival.

The Intrinsic Value of Ramsay's Work

Ramsay was not a great poet, and no one would claim that status for him. Still, his achievement was quite extraordinary and has generally been underrated in the twentieth century. His reputation has suffered for two very different reasons. Like Fergusson, he was eclipsed by the immense figure of Burns, and has come to be seen in literary histories merely as a "forerunner," seldom as a poet in his own right, a man who is important only because he happened to have influenced Burns. This perspective, obviously, is unfair to Ramsay. Secondly, he has suffered from an attitude toward him on the part of several critics that can only be called condescending. Like Burns, Ramsay had very little formal education, and that fact has sometimes been held against him by learned commentators. The outrageous snob Pinkerton went so far as to call him a "buffoon," and although such a charge can be discounted as wholly absurd, the attitude behind it has continued to taint views of Ramsay even in more recent times. Henderson, for example, sees him chiefly as a "comic satirist of low life" with "a strong vein of clever clownish humour";[5] Burns Martin sums him up as "a shrewd, gay, vulgar, kindly, thrifty, observant person with a 'knack' for versifying."[6] Such comments suggest a view of Ramsay as a kind of cozy Edinburgh "character," amusing, but not of much account as a poet. Surely Ramsay deserves better than that; as John W. Oliver says, he deserves to be respected as "a very able and accomplished man, who loved his country and did it most notable service."[7]

Ramsay's verse, like that of most poets, is very uneven in quality. Perhaps part of the problem in critical attitudes toward him is that Ramsay is very easy to depreciate: his worst poems are atrocious. But he should, of course, be judged by his best work, and that is substantial and admirable.

In the area of Scots satire he was especially prolific and impressive. His continuations of "Christis Kirk," especially canto 2, are skillful, boisterous social satires of rustic life. "A Tale of Three Bonnets," a strangely neglected and underrated work, is a solid and daring political satire; and in religious satire we have the brilliant "Marrow Ballad." Best of all are Ramsay's town satires, especially his accomplished elegies on John Cowper, Lucky Wood, and Patie Birnie, and the brilliantly imaginative "Last Speech of a Wretched Miser." In the new genre of the Scots verse epistle, his "Answer III" to Hamilton of Gilbertfield and those to Duncan Forbes and John Gay are very fine; and at least one of his many adaptations of Horatian odes, the one beginning "Look up to *Pentland's* towring Taps," is a small masterpiece.

A substantial proportion of Ramsay's work in modern Scots pastoralism, a genre that he in fact created, is very well done, including the pastoral elegies on Prior and Gay, and the love eclogue of "Patie and Roger." The last mentioned is, indeed, the most accomplished sustained piece of Scots verse in all of Ramsay's writings. *The Gentle Shepherd,* of course, as his longest and most famous production, is a major achievement; its hackneyed plot has not significantly detracted from the pleasing freshness and charm of this pastoral comedy after the passage of two and a half centuries. Of the scores of lyrics that Ramsay composed for Scots tunes a large majority, as we have seen, are mediocre or worse; but a half dozen or so of the very best— "Up in the Air," "The Widow," "Jenny Nettles," "The Cock Laird," "The Young Laird and Edinburgh Katy," "Lochaber no more," "My Peggy is a young Thing," and perhaps one or two others—are of a very high merit. Finally, in the field of narrative verse Ramsay performed well. Among his imitations of Middle Scots "The Vision" deserves more credit than it has received. A few of his renderings of the French fables into vivacious Scots are quite excellent; and in "The Monk and the Miller's Wife" and "The Miller and his Man" Ramsay produced the best verse tales in Scots of the eighteenth century before "Tam o' Shanter."

Literary criticism, at least in this century, has not dealt kindly with Ramsay; on the whole he has been underestimated. In his best work Ramsay showed more than a "knack," he gave evidence of impressive and versatile talent. In the history of Scottish poetry he has a very prominent place as *the* pioneer of the eighteenth-century revival. In British literary history he remains, of course, a minor figure, but one of absorbing interest from several points of view—especially as a satirist and as a pastoral poet.

Ramsay's contemporaries loved and respected him as "honest Allan," and he fully deserved the statue his countrymen erected in his honor in the Princes Street Gardens of Edinburgh. "Auld Reekie," the town that he loved and celebrated, still remembers him; for he was a man of whom all Scots can and should be proud. We, too, in the late twentieth century, can still read him with pleasure, and wonder at the busy, productive life that he led, at his extraordinary versatility, brightness, and energy. Allan Ramsay was an admirable man and, at his best, a remarkably good poet.

Notes and References

Chapter One

1. This phrase seems to have been first used in the form of "honest Allie" by William Hamilton of Gilbertfield in his "Epistle II" to Allan Ramsay, dated 24 July 1719. See *The Works of Allan Ramsay,* ed. Burns Martin and John W. Oliver, Scottish Text Society (Edinburgh, 1945), 1:123. This edition of Ramsay's works, incomparably the best, is used as the basic text of his writings throughout this study. The edition is in six volumes in the publications of the Scottish Text Society, 3d ser., nos. 19 (1945), 20 (1946), and 29 (1961); 4th ser., nos. 6 (1970), 7 (1972), and 8 (1974). The first two volumes are edited by Burns Martin and John W. Oliver, the last four by Alexander M. Kinghorn and Alexander Law. Hereafter all quotations from Ramsay are taken from this edition and cited as *STS,* with volume and page reference following.

2. Several useful books on the general history of Scottish literature are available, including (in chronological order) the following: Thomas F. Henderson, *Scottish Vernacular Literature,* 3d. ed. (Edinburgh, 1910); John H. Millar, *A Literary History of Scotland* (London, 1903); James Kinsley, ed., *Scottish Poetry: A Critical Survey* (London, 1955); Kurt Wittig, *The Scottish Tradition in Literature* (Edinburgh, 1958); David Craig, *Scottish Literature and the Scottish People* (London, 1961); John Speirs, *The Scots Literary Tradition,* rev. ed. (London, 1962); and, most recently, Maurice Lindsay, *History of Scottish Literature* (London, 1977).

3. For a detailed history of this genre, see Allan H. MacLaine, "The *Christis Kirk* Tradition: Its Evolution in Scots Poetry to Burns," *Studies in Scottish Literature,* 2 (1964–65):3–18, 111–24, 163–82, 234–50.

4. See Matthew P. McDiarmid, ed., *The Poems of Robert Fergusson,* Scottish Text Society (Edinburgh, 1954), 1:118.

5. See Burns's letter to Dr. John Moore, 2 August 1787, in *The Letters of Robert Burns,* ed. J. De Lancey Fergusson (Oxford, 1931), 1:106–7.

6. The earliest important biographical and critical commentary on Ramsay dates from about 1800 and was the work of George Chalmers and Alexander Fraser Tytler, Lord Woodhouselee; for their essays see *The Poems of Allan Ramsay,* 2 vols. (London, 1800) and *The Works*

of Allan Ramsay, 3 vols. (London, 1848). The modern study of Ramsay's life begins with Andrew Gibson, *New Light on Allan Ramsay* (Edinburgh, 1927), followed by Burns Martin, *Allan Ramsay: A Study of his Life and Works* (Cambridge, Mass., 1931). All of these works are subsumed, with added documentary evidence, in Alexander M. Kinghorn's "Biographical" essay in *STS,* 4:1–76, which is, on the whole, the best account of Ramsay's life yet to appear.

7. The "Cross-Well" was a public water supply in the High Street a short distance to the east of the Mercat Cross, the focal point of Edinburgh's commercial life; the "Luckenbooths" were a range of tall, narrow buildings constructed in the middle of the High Street opposite St. Giles, slightly to the west of the Cross. All three (Cross-Well, Mercat Cross, and Luckenbooths) were demolished in the early nineteenth century as obstructions to traffic. Ramsay's shop in the east end of the Luckenbooths continued to function as a bookstore and as the center of Edinburgh's literary world for long after his death. It is pleasing to know that this famous shop was later acquired by William Creech, the publisher of the first Edinburgh edition of Burns's *Poems* (1787).

8. The sheer bulk of the poetry that Ramsay left unpublished during his lifetime can easily be indicated by the page numbers in the *STS* edition: it occupies 3:149–346 and 4:259–77—nearly 220 pages.

Chapter Two

1. *The Works of Allan Ramsay* (Edinburgh, 1848), 1:60–64; this essay is hereinafter referred to as Woodhouselee.

2. See Martin, *Allan Ramsay,* 54; Daiches, "Eighteenth-Century Vernacular Poetry," in *Scottish Poetry: A Critical Survey,* ed. James Kinsley (London, 1955), 155–56; and Craig, *Scottish Literature,* 21, 37, 99.

3. For bibliographical details on the early history of this poem, see MacLaine, "The *Christis Kirk* Tradition," 14, 117–18.

4. For full bibliographical data on Gibson's edition, see William Geddie, *A Bibliography of Middle Scots Poets,* Scottish Text Society, no. 61 (Edinburgh, 1912), 96.

5. Craig, *Scottish Literature,* 23, seems to make the same mistake.

6. The marginal gloss, used here and throughout, defines the hard words in each line in their contexts. The reader's common sense will enable him to determine which words or phrases are being defined in each instance. Ramsay habitually capitalized all nouns and italicized all proper names; the capitals, italics, and (occasionally) small capitals in the quotations are Ramsay's, and have no relationship to the gloss.

7. See Woodhouselee, 82.

8. See *The Poems and Songs of Robert Burns,* ed. James Kinsley, 3 vols. (Oxford, 1968), 562. All quotations from Burns's poetical works in this book are taken from this standard edition; since all three volumes are paged consecutively only page numbers are given. This particular parallel is noted in *STS,* 6:105.

9. For details on the early history of this stanza, see Allan H. MacLaine, "New Light on the Genesis of the Burns Stanza," *Notes and Queries* 198 (August 1953):349–51; reprinted in *Burns Chronicle,* 3d ser., 3 (1954):48–51.

10. For the full text of Sempill's poem, see *The Poems of the Sempills of Beltrees,* ed. James Paterson (Edinburgh, 1849), 41–44.

11. For helpful discussions of the dating and bibliographical problems, see *STS,* 6:24–25, 45–46.

12. Burns echoes this phrase verbatim in "Tam Samson's Elegy," line 59 (*Poems,* 274); Kinsley notes the parallel in *Poems,* 1198.

13. John C. Weston, "Robert Burns's Satires," *Scottish Literary Journal* 1, no. 2 (December 1974):22.

14. Compare, for example, Burns's third stanza, in *Poems,* 439:

Ye hills, near neebors o' the starns,	*neighbors; stars*
That proudly cock your cresting cairns;	*rock piles*
Ye cliffs, the haunts of sailing yearns,	*eagles*
Where Echo slumbers:	
Come join, ye Nature's sturdiest bairns,	*children*
My wailing numbers.	

15. See Burns, *Poems,* 441–42, 275–76.

16. See *The Poems of Robert Fergusson,* ed. Matthew P. McDiarmid, Scottish Text Society, 3d ser., 21, 24 (Edinburgh, 1954, 1956), 2:67.

17. See Burns, *Poems,* 202, 1156 (Kinsley's note on the parallel).

18. For these two passages in Burns, see *Poems,* 202 and 276 respectively; neither of these instances of Ramsay's influence on Burns has been noticed before.

19. For the text of "Bonny Heck" see George Eyre-Todd, ed., *Scottish Poetry of the Eighteenth Century* (London, n.d.), 1:30–34.

20. Burns, *Poems,* 32–34.

21. Kinghorn and Law in *STS,* 6:67, point out that in an early draft of the poem in the Egerton MS Ramsay gave it two tentative titles: "The Last Speach of John Motypack . . ." and "The Dying Words of Lawrie Linkumdeedle. . . ." Both of these names, however, strike one as jocular coinages rather than the names of real persons.

22. Woodhouselee, 1:57–58, and Maurice Lindsay, *History of Scot-*

tish Literature, 176, praise the poem briefly and quote from it, but most of the critics and literary historians give it only the most cursory treatment if they mention it at all.
    23. Lindsay, *History of Scottish Literature,* 172.
    24. For helpful background on the "Marrow Controversy" see the notes in *STS,* 6:151–52, on this poem and on "Mr Ebenezer Erskins Protest" and "On George Whitefield The Strolling Preacher."
    25. Here, as in most of his unpublished poems, Ramsay is very careless about punctuation and capitalization.

Chapter Three

    1. The influence of Prior's epistle on Ramsay is convincingly argued by Carol McGuirk in "Augustan Influences on Allan Ramsay," *Studies in Scottish Literature* 16 (1981):100–102.
    2. The entire development of the Scots verse epistle in the eighteenth century from the Hamilton-Ramsay correspondence to the epistles of Burns is traced by John C. Weston in a valuable and judicious essay, "Robert Burns' Use of the Scots Verse-Epistle Form," *Philogical Quarterly* 49 (1970):188–210. Weston stresses the limitations in content of the form as originated by Hamilton and Ramsay, its modification by Fergusson, and its enormous and vital expansion in the hands of Burns as a vehicle for self-revelation.
    3. This is a reference to Gavin Douglas (ca. 1475–1522) who was bishop of Dunkeld and the author of a great translation of Virgil's *Aeneid* into Middle Scots.
    4. Hamilton's epistles were regularly included along with Ramsay's "Answers" in collected editions of Ramsay's poems from the first edition (1721) onward. The second epistle from Gilbertfield, especially, had a strong effect on Burns. Hamilton's rhymes in his opening stanza ("Epistle," "whistle," "Fistle"), for example, seem to have inspired the final stanza of Burns's "Epistle to John Lapraik" (*Poems,* 89); and his "Skellums," "Bellums" rhyme (ll. 88, 90) crops up, slightly modified to "skellum," "blellum," in Burns's "Tam o' Shanter," ll. 19, 20 (*Poems,* 558). Similarly, Hamilton's "honest *Allie*" (l. 43) is echoed in Burns's "come forrit [forward], honest Allan!" in "Sketch," l. 32 (*Poems* 192).
    5. See Fergusson, *Poems,* 2:223.
    6. Daiches, "Eighteenth-Century Vernacular Poetry," 163, notes that the form is identical to that of a Middle Scots poem, "The Claith Merchant," in the Bannatyne MS, a piece that Ramsay printed in *The Ever Green.*
    7. Burns, *Poems,* 297–99.
    8. See ibid., 762–63, 65–69, respectively.

9. Antoine Houdart De La Motte (1672–1731) was the author of *Fables* (Paris, 1719). This one, "Les Deux Livres," is book 4, fable 9.

10. See Fergusson, *Poems,* 2:210–14, 122–26, 141–45, respectively; and Burns, *Poems,* 280–89.

11. Burns, *Poems,* 248–51.

12. Ibid., 276; this parallel is noted by Kinsley, ibid., 1198.

13. For background information on this extraordinary affair, see *STS,* 6:119–20.

14. For the publication history of this epistle, see *STS,* 6:150–51.

15. Martin, *Allan Ramsay,* 62, referring to Ramsay's acknowledgment in his "Preface" to *Poems* (1721), in *STS,* 1:xviii.

16. Four additional renderings of Horace, *Odes,* book 1, odes 4–7, Ramsay left unpublished (for texts see *STS,* 3:340–43). Kinghorn in *STS,* 4:112–14, comments briefly on these, but all of them are rather trivial efforts.

17. See note in *STS,* 6:52.

18. For the evidence on this identification, see *STS,* 6:51.

19. See, for example, "Horace to Virgil," based on *Odes,* book 1, ode 3, and "The Conclusion," a rendering of Horace's *Epistles,* book 1, epistle 20, in *STS,* 1:220–22, and 245–46, in addition to the four unpublished odes referred to above in note 16.

Chapter Four

1. For an interesting discussion of the linguistic influence of Gay upon Ramsay's Scots pastorals, see McGuirk, "Augustan Influences on Allan Ramsay," 98–100.

2. There is a puzzling inconsistency in the notes by Kinghorn and Law (*STS,* 6:49) on this poem. They state that Mary Keith, the subject of the elegy, died in 1721, and then go on to say that Ramsay's poem was first published in 1720.

3. For example, two of Ramsay's phrases are paralleled verbatim by his successors: Ramsay's "Daft Gowk" (line 103) is repeated in the opening line of Fergusson's "On seeing a Butterfly" (*Poems,* 2:154); and his "to snuff the cauller Air" (line 11) crops up in Burns's "The Holy Fair," line 4 (*Poems,* 129)

4. In *STS* this poem is not printed separately, but only as incorporated in *The Gentle Shepherd,* act 1, scene 2. For the text see *STS,* 2:218–24, and for notes on the slight revisions Ramsay made from the pamphlet edition, *STS,* 6:97–100.

5. For a useful compendium of critical opinions on *The Gentle Shepherd* from 1772 to 1848, including the remarks of these three,

see *The Gentle Shepherd,* ed. William Tennant (New York, 1852), lxi–lxxii.

6. Woodhouselee, 1:88–114.

7. Tennant, ed., *Gentle Shepherd,* xxv.

8. Henderson, *Scottish Vernacular Literature,* 409–10.

9. See Daiches, "Eighteenth-Century Vernacular Poetry," 162–64; Lindsay, *History of Scottish Literature,* 177–78; and Kinghorn in *STS,* 4:90–108.

10. Thomas Crawford, *Society and the Lyric: A Study of the Song Culture of Eighteenth-Century Scotland* (Edinburgh, 1979), 70–96.

11. See ibid., 70–78; also Kinghorn in *STS,* 4:90–92; and McGuirk, "Augustan Influences on Allan Ramsay," 98–100.

12. See especially Philips, *Third Pastoral* and *Fourth Pastoral* (London, 1708).

13. *The Works of Thomas Purney,* ed. H. O. White (Oxford, 1933).

14. "Neps" is an amusing example of the peculiar Scots fondness for nicknames and diminutives. "Neps" is a shortened form of "Eppie," which is a diminutive of "Elspa" or "Elspeth," which in turn is the Scots variant form of "Elizabeth."

15. Compare, e.g., act 2, scene 2, in any edition of Steele's play.

16. See ibid., act 1, scene 2.

17. See Burns, *Poems,* 137–45.

18. See ibid., 557–64, 167–72, 79–84. Compare, especially, *The Gentle Shepherd,* 2.3.31–50, and 5.1.26–47, 62–75, with "Tam o' Shanter," lines 89–104, 115–42, 166–70.

19. See act 5, scene 3.

20. Crawford, *Society and the Lyric,* 94–95.

21. Ibid., 82.

Chapter Five

1. Crawford, *Society and the Lyric,* 174.

2. Fergusson, *Poems,* 2:91.

3. Burns, *Poems,* 42.

4. Ibid., 795–96, 384, respectively.

5. See Daiches, "Eighteenth-Century Vernacular Poetry," 161–62, and Crawford, *Society and the Lyric,* 175–76.

6. Burns, *Poems,* 804.

7. Ibid., 200–201.

8. For the texts of these songs see ibid., 384, 184; Kinsley notes both parallels, 1261, 1139.

9. Ibid., 879.

10. Daiches, "Eighteenth-Century Vernacular Poetry," 162.

11. Burns, *Poems,* 204.

12. *The Merry Muses of Caledonia,* ed. James Barke and Sydney Goodsir Smith (Edinburgh, 1959), 122.

13. There is a version in Ramsay's handwriting in the Egerton MS 2023; see *STS,* 6:108.

14. For a full and illuminating note on the literary and folk background, see Kinsley in Burns, *Poems,* 1392–93.

15. Kinghorn and Law in *STS* simply accept the song as Ramsay's without comment or proof; so does Crawford, *Society and the Lyric,* 24–25. Kenneth Buthlay, on the other hand, thinks it is "an old song"—see his essay in *Scottish Literary Journal* 2 (July 1975):50.

16. Crawford, *Society and the Lyric,* 115.

17. See Burns, *Poems,* 54–56, 441–42.

18. For an interesting analysis of this song contrasted with Ramsay's weak version of "Auld Lang Syne," see McGuirk, "Augustan Influences on Allan Ramsay," 106–8.

19. Burns, *Poems,* 195–209; see also Kinsley's note, 1149, and *STS,* 6:107–8.

20. See Burns, *Poems,* 850, and Kinsley's note, 1505–6.

21. Daiches, "Eighteenth-Century Vernacular Poetry," 162.

22. Burns, *Poems,* 422.

Chapter Six

1. See Hailes, *Ancient Scottish Poems* (Edinburgh, 1770), and Pinkerton, *Ancient Scotish Poems* (Edinburgh, 1786).

2. Daiches, "Eighteenth-Century Vernacular Poetry," 167, interprets the fable as an anti-English allegory, though the evidence for this view is not apparent in the text.

3. For evidence of Ramsay's changes in Lady Wardlaw's spelling, see *STS,* 6:193.

4. See, for example, "The Poet's Wish" (*STS,* 1:243–44) or "To the Whin-Bush Club" (*STS,* 1:211–12).

5. See Burns, *Poems,* 103–13, and Kinsley's full treatment of Burns's sources, 1069–74.

6. Lindsay, *History of Scottish Literature,* 179, for example, calls it "an absurdly pseudo–Middle Scots poem."

7. See Antoine Houdart De La Motte, *Fables* (Paris, 1719); and Jean de La Fontaine, *Fables,* books 1–6 (Paris, 1668), books 7–11 (Paris, 1678–79), book 12 (Paris, 1694). For specific identification of the sources of Ramsay's individual fables in La Motte and La Fontaine, see *STS,* 6:61–66, 117–19, 140.

8. In the second edition of *Poems,* vol. 2.

9. See *STS,* 6:85–86.

10. Martin, *Allan Ramsay,* 66.

11. Burns, *Poems*, 557–64.
12. It may be noted here that as in most of his unpublished poems Ramsay took few pains with capitalization.

Chapter Seven

1. See Craig, *Scottish Literature*, 235–50 and passim.
2. Daiches, "Eighteenth-Century Vernacular Poetry," 161.
3. For this identification, see *STS*, 6:108.
4. Burns, *Poems*, 42–43. For identifications of the many other sources of Burns's song, see Otto Ritter, *Quellenstudien zu Robert Burns* (Berlin, 1901), 23–26; Thomas Crawford, *Burns: A Study of the Poems and Songs* (Stanford, Calif., 1960), 9–12; and Kinsley in Burns, *Poems*, 1022–23.
5. For an account of Aikman's life, see *STS*, 6:209.

Chapter Eight

1. For the texts of these two sets of songs, see *STS*, 1:38–52, 167–75; and for bibliographical data on them, *STS*, 6:29–30, 44.
2. See *STS*, 6:189.
3. For bibliographical data on all of these editions, see *STS*, 6:7–15.
4. For information on Ramsay's collaborators, see *STS*, 4:143, and Daiches, "Eighteenth-Century Vernacular Poetry," 167–68, 311–13.
5. See Kinsley's bibliographical notes in Burns, *Poems*, 997.
6. Hailes, *Ancient Scottish Poems*; Pinkerton, *Ancient Scotish Poems*.
7. Daiches ("Eighteenth-Century Vernacular Poetry," 166), for example, after quoting the "Postscript," says: "To which monstrous conclusion Ramsay calmly appends the words, 'Quod Dunbar,' " implying that Ramsay was attempting to foist off his own pedestrian stanzas as part of the original poem.

Chapter Nine

1. Henderson, *Scottish Vernacular Literature*, 410.
2. See Daiches, "Eighteenth-Century Vernacular Poetry," 164; and Kinghorn, *STS*, 4:128.
3. See "To Mr. Robert Fergusson," by "J. S.," dated "Berwick, August 31, 1772," in Fergusson's *Poems*, 2:69.
4. Burns recorded this judgment in his *First Commonplace Book* in the entry for August 1785. The full text of this passage can be found conveniently cited in Franklyn B. Snyder, *The Life of Robert Burns* (New York, 1932), 88.

5. Henderson, *Scottish Vernacular Literature,* 406.
6. Martin, *Allan Ramsay,* 72.
7. John W. Oliver, "The Eighteenth Century Revival," in *Edinburgh Essays on Scots Literature* (Edinburgh, 1933), 96.

Selected Bibliography

PRIMARY SOURCES

This list, arranged chronologically, is limited to first editions of Ramsay's collected writings and anthologies, editions of special historic interest, and the most recent, definitive editions of his works and those of his followers, Fergusson and Burns.

Poems. Edinburgh, 1721.
Fables and Tales. Edinburgh, 1722.
The Tea-Table Miscellany. Vol. 1. Edinburgh, 1723.
The Ever Green. 2 vols. Edinburgh, 1724.
The Gentle Shepherd. Edinburgh, 1725.
The Tea-Table Miscellany. Vol. 2. Edinburgh, 1726.
The Tea-Table Miscellany. Vol. 3. Edinburgh, 1727.
Poems. Vol. 2. Edinburgh, 1728.
Collection of Thirty Fables. Edinburgh, 1730.
A Collection of Scots Proverbs. Edinburgh, 1737.
The Tea-Table Miscellany. Vol. 4. Edinburgh, 1737.
The Poems of Allan Ramsay. Edited, with life of Ramsay, by George Chalmers, and critical essay by Alexander Fraser Tytler, Lord Woodhouselee. 2 vols. London, 1800.
The Works of Allan Ramsay. Edited, with life of the author, by George Chalmers, and an essay on his genius and writings by Lord Woodhouselee. 3 vols. London, 1848.
The Works of Allan Ramsay. 6 vols. Scottish Text Society, 3d ser., nos. 19–20, 29; 4th ser., nos. 6–8. Edinburgh: William Blackwood, 1945–74. Vols. 1–2 edited by Burns Martin and John W. Oliver; vols. 3–6 by Alexander M. Kinghorn and Alexander Law. This is the definitive scholarly edition of Ramsay, incomparably superior to anything previously published.
The Poems of Robert Fergusson. Edited, with life, criticism, and notes, by Matthew P. McDiarmid. 2 vols. Scottish Text Society, 3d ser., nos. 21, 24. Edinburgh: William Blackwood, 1954, 1956. The standard modern edition.
The Poems and Songs of Robert Burns. Edited, with extensive commentary,

by James Kinsley. 3 vols. Oxford: Clarendon Press, 1968. The
standard modern edition.

SECONDARY SOURCES

1. Bibliography
The most complete bibliography of Ramsay's writings is to be found
in the Scottish Text Society edition of his *Works* (vol. 6) listed above,
which incorporates the contents of Burns Martin's *A Bibliography of
the Writings of Allan Ramsay* (Glasgow Bibliographical Society, vol.
10 [Glasgow, 1931]).

2. General Studies of Scots Literature
Craig, David. *Scottish Literature and the Scottish People, 1680–1830.*
London: Chatto & Windus, 1961. An interesting study with considerable attention to Ramsay, especially with respect to his use
of the Scots language.
Crawford, Thomas. *Society and the Lyric: A Study of the Song Culture
of Eighteenth-Century Scotland.* Edinburgh: Scottish Academic Press,
1979. A judicious and comprehensive study of Scots song, with
extensive comment on Ramsay.
Graham, Henry Grey. *Scottish Men of Letters in the Eighteenth Century.*
London: A. & C. Black, 1901. An older work, but still valuable,
especially on minor writers.
Henderson, Thomas Finlayson. *Scottish Vernacular Literature.* 3d ed.
Edinburgh: John Grant, 1910. A comprehensive work, still useful,
though the section on Ramsay is too brief and does him less
than justice.
Kinsley, James, ed. *Scottish Poetry: A Critical Survey.* London: Cassell,
1955. An excellent volume of essays by various hands.
Lindsay, Maurice. *History of Scottish Literature.* London: Robert Hale,
1977. The most recent and comprehensive book on the subject;
section on Ramsay is brief but generally adequate.
Speirs, John. *The Scots Literary Tradition.* Rev. ed., London: Chatto
& Windus, 1962. A solid, interesting short book.
Wittig, Kurt. *The Scottish Tradition in Literature.* Edinburgh: Oliver
& Boyd, 1958. A valuable general book that attempts to define
the distinctive qualities of Scots literature.

3. Biographical and Critical Studies
Chalmers, George. "Life of the Author." In *Poems of Allan Ramsay.*
London, 1800. The first significant biography of the poet.

Crawford, Thomas. "The Gentle Shepherd." In *Society and the Lyric* (listed above). A substantial chapter on Ramsay's pastoral play, balanced and convincing.

Daiches, David. "Eighteenth-Century Vernacular Poetry." In *Scottish Poetry: A Critical Survey* (listed above). Contains one of the best modern treatments of Ramsay's poetry, generally comprehensive and judicious.

Gibson, Andrew. *New Light on Allan Ramsay.* Edinburgh: W. Brown, 1927. This is the pioneer modern study of Ramsay's life and bibliography, superseded by Burns Martin (see below).

Hailes, Lord, ed. *Ancient Scottish Poems.* Edinburgh, 1770. Contains unfavorable comments on Ramsay's editorial methods in *The Ever Green.*

Kinghorn, Alexander M. "Biographical and Critical Introduction." In vol. 4 of the Scottish Text Society edition of the *Works* of Ramsay (listed above). This is the most extensive piece of Ramsay biography and criticism yet to appear. The biography is the best available, incorporating the results of Burns Martin's work (see below) with additional evidence. The critical sections are generally very good, but are incomplete, concentrating on Ramsay's pastoral poetry, his "translations" from French and Latin, and his editorial labors, but skipping over his Scots satires, epistles, and other important genres.

MacLaine, Allan H. "The *Christis Kirk* Tradition: Its Evolution in Scots Poetry to Burns." *Studies in Scottish Literature* 2 (1964–65):3–18, 111–24, 163–82, 234–50. Contains detailed treatment of Ramsay's role in the history of this genre.

Martin, Burns. *Allan Ramsay: A Study of his Life and Works.* Cambridge, Mass.: Harvard University Press, 1931. The best biography prior to Kinghorn. The critical commentary is relatively brief but sound.

McGuirk, Carol. "Augustan Influences on Allan Ramsay." *Studies in Scottish Literature* 16 (1981):97–109. Interesting study of the effect of English poets, especially Prior, Gay, Pope, and Ambrose Philips, upon Ramsay's work.

Oliver, John W. "The Eighteenth Century Revival." In *Edinburgh Essays on Scots Literature.* Edinburgh: Edinburgh University Press, 1933, pp. 78–104. This essay, devoted largely to Ramsay, is sympathetic and solid.

Pinkerton, John, ed. *Ancient Scotish Poems.* Edinburgh, 1786. Contains outrageously unfair comments on Ramsay by an intellectual snob.

Tennant, William. "Remarks on the Writings of Allan Ramsay." In *The Gentle Shepherd.* New York, 1852, pp. xxv–xxx. A brief, high laudatory estimate of Ramsay's work.

Weston, John C. "Robert Burns' Use of the Scots Verse-Epistle Form." *Philological Quarterly* 49 (1970):188–210. An excellent essay, with detailed discussion of the roles of Ramsay and Hamilton of Gilbertfield in creating this genre.

Woodhouselee, Alexander Fraser Tytler, Lord. "Essay on the Genius and Writings of Allan Ramsay." In *Poems of Allan Ramsay.* London, 1800. The first extensive critical treatment of Ramsay's poetry, enthusiastic but generally sound.

Zenzinger, Peter. *My Muse is British: Allan Ramsay und die Neubelebung der Schottischen Dichtkunst im 18. Jahrhundert.* Series: Beiträge zur Anglistik, 1. Grossen-Linden, West Germany: Hoffman Verlag, 1977. This is a major and valuable piece of Ramsay scholarship, of which the present writer became aware too late, unfortunately, to take account of in this study. Zenzinger's work is primarily a contribution to cultural history rather than to literary criticism, focusing chiefly upon the political, cultural, and social backgrounds to Ramsay's poetry and the Scots revival.

Index

Addison, Joseph, 8, 59–61, 80
Aikman, William, 121
Arbuthnot, Dr. John, 52
"Auld Lang Syne," 83, 119
"Auld Rob Morris," 127
"Auld Wife beyont the Fire, The,"
127

Baliol, John, 103–104
Bannatyne Manuscript (1568), 10, *15–16*,
59, 100, 110, 124, 129–32
Barbour, John: *The Bruce*, 1, 2
Beattie, James, 68
Blair, Hugh, 68
Blind Harry, 2; *Wallace*, 5
"Blythsome Bridal, The," 127
"Bonny Barbara Allan," 128
Burchett, Josiah, 60, 65
Burns, Robert, 2, 8, 20, 30, 32, 35, 41–
43, 50, 58, 65, 68, 78–79, 81–84, 86,
92, 99, 114, 119, 125–26, 128, *133–*
39; "Address to the Deil," 76; "Brigs
of Ayr, The," 51; "Death and Dr.
Hornbook," 76; "Death and Dying
Words of Puir Mailie, The," 35; "Elegy
on Captain Matthew Henderson," 29–
30, 93, 145n14; "Epistle to a Young
Friend," 51; "Epistle to Davie," 50;
"Epistle to William Simson," 28; "Extemporare Verses on Dining with Lord
Daer," 49–50; "For the Sake of Some-
body," 96; "Halloween," 17; "Holy
Fair, The," 39; "Holy Tulzie, The," 28;
"Holy Willie's Prayer," 28; "I Love my
Jean," 98–99; "I'm o'er young to Marry
Yet," 84, 87; "Jolly Beggars, The," 31,
86, 88, 94; "Last May a Braw Wooer,"
84; "Mary Morison," 83, 120–21,
150n4; *Merry Muses of Caledonia, The,*
88; "Ordination, The," 28; "Rantin
dog the Daddie o't, The," 87; "Ronalds
of the Bennals, The," 93; "Song—For
a' that and a' that," 50; "Steer her up,
and had her gawn," 88; "Tam O'Shanter," 22, 76, 112, 140; "Tam Samson's
Elegy," 28, 30–31, 51–52; "Twa Dogs,

The," 76; "Vision, The," 103; "Wha
is that at my bower door?" 90

Carmichael, William, of Skirling, 124
Charmer, The, 124
Chatterton, Thomas, 104
Chaucer, Geoffrey, 28, 109, 112; *Friar's*
Tale, 109; *Miller's Tale,* 19, 110; *Par-*
doner's Prologue, 38; *Parlement of Fowles,*
101; *Reeve's Tale,* 112
"Christis Kirk on the Green," 2, 3, 4, 8,
15–17, 124, 132
"Christis Kirk" tradition and stanza, 2, 8,
15–17, 48, 94, 118, 135, 138
Clerk, Sir John, 56, 121
Craig, David, 15, 17, 114
Crawford, Robert, 10, 126–27
Crawford, Thomas, 68–70, 79–81, 83, 85,
91

Dacier (French translator of Horace), 54
Daiches, David, 15, 17, 21, 68, 85, 88,
96, 119, 134
Douglas, Gavin, translation of Virgil's *Ae-*
neid, 2
Dryden, John: *Absalom and Achitophel* and
MacFlecknoe, 118
Dunbar, William, 2, 3, 15, 40, 109;
"Dance of the Sevin Deidly Synnis,
The," 132; "General Satyre, A," 132;
"Golden Targe, The," 2; "Lament for
the Makaris," 130, 132; "Thistle and
the Rose, The," 132

Easy Club, 7, 123

Fergusson, Robert, 13, 20, 32, 35, 40,
42, 58, 65, 78, 114, *133–39;* "Caller
Oysters," 30; "Drink Eclogue, A," 50;
"Farmer's Ingle, The," 79; "Ghaists,
The," 50–51; "Hallow'fair," 83; "Hor-
ace, *Odes,* book 1, ode 11," 46; "Mutual
Complaint of Plainstanes and Causey,
The," 50
Forbes, John, of Newhall, 56

Index 159

Scots Songs (1720), 123
"Soger Laddie, The," 94
"Song To the Tune of, Jenny beguil'd
the Webster," 89
"Song, Tune of Lochaber no more, A,"
93–94, 99, 140
"Spring and the Syke, The," 108
"Steer her up, and had her gawn," 87–
88
"Tale of Three Bonnets, A," 8, 9, 14,
21–24, 135–36, 138, 140
"Tartana," 7, 48, 116
Tea-Table Miscellany, The, 5, 10, 82,
86–87, 93, 97, 120–21, 123–30,
133
"There's my Thumb I'll ne'er beguile
Thee," 92
"This is not mine ain House," 94–95,
99
"To His Grace John Duke of Rox-
burgh," 48
"To Josiah Burchet, Esq.," 48
"To L. M. M.," 120–21
"To Mr. Jo. Kerr of King's College,
Aberdeen," 48–49
"To Mr. William Starrat," 49
"To my kind and worthy Friends in Ire-
land," 51
"To R—— H—— B——, an Ode,"
56–57
"To the Ph—— —— an Ode," 57–
58, 140
"To the Right Honourable, William
Earl of Dalhousie," 55
"Twa Cats and the Cheese, The," 107
"Twa Cut-Purses, The," 108
"Twa Lizards, The," 105–106
"Up in the Air," 85, 99, 123, 140
"Vision, The," 100, 102–105, 113,
132, 138, 140
"Wealth, or the Woody," 55
"When first my dear laddie gade to the
green hill," 98
"Widow, The," 86–87, 99, 140
"Young Laird and Edinburgh Katy,
The," 83–84, 99, 123, 140

"Young Lass contra auld Man, The,"
89, 99

Ramsay, Allan, Jr., 12, 54
"Rantin roaring Willie," 120
"Rare Willy drown'd in Yarrow," 128
"Rob's Jock came to woo our Jenny," 127

Scott, Alexander, 2; "Justing and Debait,"
3, 15–17, 132
Scott, Sir Walter, 78, 125
Scottish National Dictionary, 137
Sempill of Beltrees, Robert: "The Life and
Death of Habbie Simson," 3, 4, 8, 24–
26, 135; "Epitaph on Sanny Briggs,"
24
"Sir Patrick Spence," 102
Steele, Sir Richard, 60–61; *The Conscious
Lovers,* 70, 73, 75, 78
Stevenson, R. L., 78
Stuart, Alexander: *Musick for Allan Ram-
say's Collection of Scots Songs,* 125
Suckling, Sir John: "Why so pale and wan,
fond lover?" 128

Tennant, William, 68
Thomson, George: *A Select Collection of
Original Scotish Airs,* 128
"Todlen butt, and todlen ben," 127

Union, Act of (1707), 4, 21, 103–104,
137

Vaughan, Henry: "The World," 117

Waller, Edmund, 115
"Waly, waly, gin love be bonny," 127
Wardlaw, Lady. "Hardy-knute," 100
102, 132
Watson, James: *A Choice Collection of Comic
and Serious Scots Poems, both Antient and
Modern,* 4, 5, 10, 16, 35, 124, 129, 135
Weston, John C., 28, 146n2
"Wife of Auchtermuchty," 132
"William and Margaret," 128
Woodhouselee, Lord, 14, 21, 68